My Book

This book belongs to

Name: _____

Grade 5

Copy right © 2019 MATH-KNOTS LLC

All rights reserved, no part of this publication may be reproduced, stored in any system or transmitted in any form, or by any means, electronic, mechanical, photocopying, recording, or otherwise without the written permission of MATH-KNOTS LLC.

Cover Design by :
Gowri Vemuri

First Edition :
August , 2023

Author :
Gowri Vemuri

Edited by :
Raksha Pothapragada

Questions: mathknots.help@gmail.com

NOTE : CCSSO or NCTM or VDOE is neither affiliated nor sponsors or endorses this product.

Dedication

This book is dedicated to:

My Mom, who is my best critic, guide and supporter.

To what I am today, and what I am going to become tomorrow,

is all because of your blessings, unconditional affection and support.

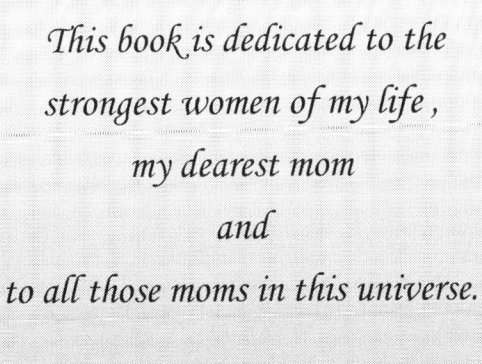

This book is dedicated to the

strongest women of my life,

my dearest mom

and

to all those moms in this universe.

G.V.

Grade 5
Index

Test No	Page No
Test 1	9-26
Test 2	27-48
Test 3	49-68
Test 4	69-86
Answer Keys	87-141

Grade 5
ELA Practice Test 1

The Magical Quern and the Salted Sea

Directions: *Read the passages and answer the questions that follow.*

Adapted from: WHY THE SEA IS SALT

1. Once upon a time, in a land far away, there lived two brothers. One was rich, and the other was poor. It was Christmas Eve, and the poor brother had nothing to celebrate the festive season. With hope in his heart, he went to his rich brother and asked for help.

2. The rich brother, though not pleased to see him, made a deal. He promised the poor brother a whole flitch of bacon if he agreed to do something for him. Desperate and grateful, the poor brother agreed without knowing what he was getting into.

3. The rich brother handed him the flitch of bacon and said, "Go straight to Hell if you want this, but there's a condition. You must bring back a magical quern from behind the Devil's door."

4. Determined to keep his word, the poor brother embarked on a long journey. After walking all day, he stumbled upon a bright light. Curious, he approached and met an old man with a long white beard. The man revealed that he was in Hell and offered advice to the poor brother.

5. Entering Hell, the poor brother found himself surrounded by devils eager to buy the flitch of bacon. He agreed to sell it but demanded the hand-quern behind the door as payment. Reluctantly, the Devil agreed, and the poor brother received the quern.

6. On his way back, the poor brother learned how to use the quern, which could grind almost anything. Arriving home late on Christmas Eve, he surprised his wife with the magical quern's abilities. They feasted on an abundance of food and invited friends and family to celebrate.

7. The rich brother, consumed by envy, begged to have the quern. Eventually, he persuaded his brother to lend it to him until hay-harvest, promising a hefty sum. However, the poor brother never taught him how to use it.

8. When the rich brother brought the quern home, he commanded it to grind herrings and broth. The quern obeyed, but it couldn't be stopped. The kitchen flooded, and the broth flowed into the parlour. Fleeing for his life, the rich brother warned his wife about the calamity.

9. Meanwhile, the poor brother's wife grew concerned and went home. On her way, she encountered the overflowing broth, herrings, and bread rushing down the road. Astonished, she realized the trouble her husband had escaped.

10. The rich brother rushed to return the quern, fearing the destruction it could cause. He paid an additional sum, and the poor brother regained possession of the quern. With its power, he transformed their lives, building a golden house and earning fame across the land.

11. One day, a skipper came seeking the quern's ability to grind salt. The skipper convinced the poor brother to sell it, but he didn't learn how to control it. As the quern ground salt endlessly, the ship sank, and the quern remains at the bottom of the sea, grinding salt to this day, explaining why the sea is salty.

Grade 5

ELA Practice Test 1

1. Why did the poor brother go to his rich brother on Christmas Eve?

    A) To celebrate the festive season together

    B) To ask for help

    C) To exchange gifts

    D) To share a meal

2. What did the rich brother promise to give the poor brother in return for a favor?

    A) A magical quern

    B) A feast for Christmas

    C) A golden house

    D) A flitch of bacon

3. Where did the poor brother find a bright light on his journey?

    A) In a dark cave

    B) In his brother's house

    C) In the Devil's dwelling

    D) In the forest

4. What is the main idea of paragraph 5?

    A) The poor brother surprises his wife with the magical quern's abilities.

    B) The poor brother encounters an old man in Hell who offers him advice.

    C) The poor brother learns how to use the quern on his way back home.

    D) The poor brother sells the flitch of bacon to devils in Hell.

5. What does the word "flitch" mean in the story of the magical quern?

    A) A type of magical object

    B) A slab of cured bacon

    C) A piece of furniture

    D) A hidden door in Hell

6. How did the poor brother surprise his wife when he returned home?

    A) With a feast prepared by the quern

    B) With a sack of gold coins

    C) With a beautiful golden house

    D) With a magical creature

7. Why did the rich brother want to borrow the quern from his poor brother?

    A) To build a golden house

    B) To learn its magical abilities

    C) To impress his friends and family

    D) To grind salt for his ship

8. Which paragraph in the story of the magical quern could have the heading "The Envious Brother"?

    A) Paragraph 4

    B) Paragraph 6

    C) Paragraph 7

    D) Paragraph 9

9. What became of the quern in the end?

    A) It was destroyed by the rich brother

    B) It was returned to the poor brother's house

    C) It was lost during the flood

    D) It continued grinding salt at the bottom of the sea

The Nightingale and The Rose

1. Once upon a time, there was a young student who wished to dance with his beloved. She had promised to dance with him if he brought her red flowers, but sadly, his garden did not have any.

2. A Nightingale, perched on a nearby tree, heard his sadness and felt sorry for him. Filled with kindness, the Nightingale thought of the young student as a true lover.

3. Night after night, she had sung about him without knowing him, sharing his story with the stars. The Nightingale saw how much he longed for a red flower, which he believed would bring him joy. Even though he was wise and knowledgeable, not having a red flower troubled him deeply.

4. The Nightingale thought about the power of love, realizing the student's genuine passion. Love, she understood, was an incredible and priceless force that was more important than material things. Determined to help the student, she decided to find a red flower for him.

5. Flying through the garden, the Nightingale discovered a rosebush in the middle of the grassy area. She asked it to give her a red flower in exchange for her sweetest song. Sadly, the rosebush could only offer white flowers.

6. Undeterred, the Nightingale approached another rosebush near the old sun-dial, but it only had yellow flowers to offer.

7. Finally, the Nightingale went to a rosebush beneath the student's window. She begged it for a red flower but received a sad answer. The rosebush's branches had been damaged by winter storms, leaving it without any flowers. However, it revealed a secret way to create a red flower: the Nightingale had to make it from music in the moonlight and color it with her own heart's blood.

8. Knowing the terrible price she had to pay, the Nightingale accepted the challenge, believing that love was more precious than life itself. With great dedication, she pressed her chest against a thorn and sang all night long. The pain grew stronger, but she kept going, singing about the birth of love and the essence of passion.

9. As dawn approached, the Nightingale's song reached its climax, and the flower on the rosebush transformed from pale to deep red. Yet, the Nightingale grew weaker, and she could not withstand the thorn's piercing any longer. With her last breath, she was happy, knowing the flower was complete.

10. Meanwhile, the student, unaware of the Nightingale's sacrifice, woke up and found a miraculous red flower outside his window. He was overjoyed and hurried to present it to his beloved.

11. Unfortunately, she rejected his gift, considering it less valuable than the precious jewels given to her by the Chamberlain's nephew.

12. Heartbroken and angry at her lack of appreciation, the student threw the flower into the street, where it met a tragic end under the wheel of a passing cart.

13. He retreated to his room, returning to his dusty books and abandoning the magical world of love. Little did he know that the Nightingale's sacrifice had given him the truest form of love—a flower stained with her own lifeblood, symbolizing the depth and sincerity that he had failed to understand.

-Adapted from The Rose and The Nightingale

10. What did the student's beloved demand in order to dance with him?

    A) Red roses

    B) White flowers

    C) Yellow flowers

    D) Precious jewels

11. Why did the Nightingale decide to help the student?

    A) Because she wanted to become his friend

    B) Because she wanted him to sing with her

    C) Because she felt sorry for him

    D) Because she wanted to find a red flower for herself

12. What did the Nightingale have to do to create a red flower?

   A) Sing her sweetest song to a rosebush

   B) Exchange her feathers for a red flower

   C) Ask the Chamberlain's nephew for a red flower

   D) Make a flower from music and her own heart's blood

13. What did the student do when his beloved rejected the red flower?

   A) He thanked her for her honesty

   B) He presented her with precious jewels

   C) He threw the flower into the street

   D) He asked the Nightingale for another flower

14. How did the Nightingale's sacrifice affect the student?

   A) It made him appreciate the value of love

   B) It made him abandon logic and metaphysics

   C) It had no effect as he was unaware of the sacrifice

   D) It made him forget about his beloved

15. What did the student do after his beloved rejected the red flower?

   A) He decided to become a dancer

   B) He decided to give up on love

   C) He decided to find more red flowers

   D) He decided to write a love poem

16. Which paragraph describes the Nightingale's sacrifice?

   A) Paragraph 7

   B) Paragraph 8

   C) Paragraph 9

   D) Paragraph 10

17. What does the red flower stained with the Nightingale's lifeblood symbolize?

    A) The student's wisdom and knowledge

    B) The Chamberlain's nephew's precious jewels

    C) The student's dedication and passion for love

    D) The Nightingale's understanding of love

A Devoted Friend

1. Once upon a time, in a peaceful village, lived an honest and kind-hearted man named Hans. He resided in a tiny cottage and spent his days tending to his beautiful garden, which bloomed with an array of colorful flowers throughout the seasons. Hans had many friends, but his most devoted companion was the wealthy Miller named Hugh.

2. Hugh, the Miller, held a strong belief that true friends should share everything. He would often visit Hans and generously bring him gifts of flowers, herbs, and fruits from his own abundant resources. The Miller spoke passionately about the virtues of friendship and the importance of selflessness.

3. During the spring, summer, and autumn, Hans was content and happy. However, when winter arrived, he faced hardships. Without flowers or produce to sell, he suffered from cold and hunger. It was during this time that the Miller never visited Hans, claiming that people in trouble should be left alone.

4. Meanwhile, the Miller's family questioned his lack of assistance to Hans. The Miller dismissed their concerns, fearing that Hans might become envious if he saw their warm home and plentiful provisions. He believed that protecting Hans from temptations and preserving his contentment were the true acts of friendship.

5. When spring returned, the Miller finally decided to visit Hans. He praised Hans for the beauty of his blooming primroses and inquired about his well-being during the winter. Hans gratefully expressed his happiness, sharing his plan to sell the flowers and buy back his wheelbarrow, which he had sold to survive the harsh season.

6. Upon hearing this, the Miller offered his own dilapidated wheelbarrow to Hans as a gift. He claimed that true friendship involved acts of generosity, even if the gift was of lesser value. In return, he asked Hans for a basket full of flowers.

7. Although Hans had intended to sell the flowers, he valued the Miller's friendship more than material possessions. He gladly filled the Miller's basket, giving away all his precious primroses.

8. Days later, when Hans was nailing honeysuckle against his porch, the Miller appeared once again. This time, he requested Hans to carry a heavy sack of flour to the market for him. Despite being busy with his own chores, Hans reluctantly agreed, not wanting to appear unfriendly.

9. And so, he shouldered the heavy load and set off to the market, leaving behind his own tasks. As Hans trudged along with the weight on his shoulders, he could not help but wonder if the Miller's acts of friendship were truly reciprocal.

10. This story teaches us about the true meaning of friendship and the importance of selflessness. It illustrates how Hans, despite facing hardships, remained devoted and self-sacrificing, while the Miller's acts of friendship seemed more conditional and self-serving. In the end, true friendship is not about what one can gain, but about genuine care, support, and equality.

-Adapted from The Devoted Friend

18. Who is the protagonist of the story?

    A) Hugh

    B) The Miller

    C) Hans

    D) None of the above

19. Which two words from the story have the same suffix?

    A) kindness, selflessness

    B) generous, happiness

    C) cottage, dilapidated

    D) flowers, medicinal

20. Why did the Miller stop visiting Hans during the winter?

    A) He had become envious of Hans' garden.

    B) He had fallen ill and could not leave his home.

    C) He had moved to a different village.

    D) He believed people in trouble should be left alone.

21. What did the Miller offer Hans as a gift?

    A) A bag of flour

    B) An old wheelbarrow

    C) A basket of flowers

    D) A dilapidated cottage

22. What did Hans intend to do with the flowers he grew?

   A) Sell them in the market

   B) Decorate his cottage

   C) Give them to the Miller's family

   D) Use them for medicinal purposes

23. Why did Hans agree to carry the Miller's sack of flour?

   A) He wanted to impress the Miller.

   B) He had nothing better to do.

   C) He did not want to appear unfriendly.

   D) He needed the exercise.

24. How did Hans feel about the Miller's acts of friendship?

   A) He was grateful and appreciative.

   B) He was suspicious and doubtful.

   C) He was envious and resentful.

   D) He was indifferent and uninterested.

25. What did Hans value more than material possessions?

   A) Money and wealth

   B) Status and reputation

   C) The Miller's friendship

   D) Personal happiness and well-being

The Wonderful World of Kaleidoscopes

1. Kaleidoscope is a fascinating optical device that has captured the imagination of people for centuries. It consists of a tube with mirrors and colored glass or beads inside. When you look through the eyepiece and rotate the tube, you are treated to a mesmerizing display of ever-changing patterns and colors.

2. The word "kaleidoscope" comes from Greek words meaning "beautiful form to see." And indeed, the patterns created by a kaleidoscope are truly beautiful. They can resemble intricate mandalas, symmetrical designs, or even floral arrangements. Each turn of the tube reveals a new arrangement of colors and shapes, creating a sense of wonder and surprise.

3. The magic of a kaleidoscope lies in its mirrors. These mirrors are placed at specific angles inside the tube, creating multiple reflections of the objects inside. As the tube is rotated, the mirrors reflect and multiply the images, creating the stunning patterns we see. The colored glass or beads inside the kaleidoscope serve as the objects that create these reflections. They come in various shapes and sizes, adding to the diversity of the patterns.

4. Kaleidoscopes have been enjoyed by people of all ages. They provide a source of endless entertainment and inspiration. Children are often captivated by the kaleidoscope's ever-changing patterns, while adults appreciate its artistic and meditative qualities. Some people even collect kaleidoscopes as works of art, as there are many unique and intricately designed pieces available.

5. In addition to being a source of amusement, kaleidoscopes also have educational value. They can help develop a child's sense of color, pattern recognition, and spatial awareness. By observing the patterns formed in a kaleidoscope, one can learn about symmetry, reflection, and the principles of optics.

6. Today, kaleidoscopes come in various forms. Traditional handheld kaleidoscopes are still popular, but there are also larger kaleidoscopes that can be mounted on a stand or even displayed as decorative pieces. Some modern kaleidoscopes are even equipped with lights and rotating mechanisms, enhancing the visual experience.

7. In conclusion, kaleidoscopes are enchanting devices that bring joy and wonder to those who peer through their eyepieces. With their intricate patterns and vibrant colors, they provide a glimpse into a world of beauty and harmony. Whether as a toy, an art piece, or a tool for learning, the kaleidoscope continues to inspire and amaze people of all ages.

26. According to the passage, what is a kaleidoscope?

    A) An educational toy

    B) An optical device

    C) A decorative piece

    D) A rotating mechanism

27. In paragraph 3, how does the author help the reader understand the mechanism of a kaleidoscope?

   A) By quoting inventors

   B) By describing the materials used

   C) By explaining the principles of optics

   D) By providing historical anecdotes

28. What is the origin of the word "kaleidoscope"?

   A) Latin

   B) Greek

   C) French

   D) English

29. How do the mirrors inside a kaleidoscope contribute to the patterns?

   A) They reflect and multiply the images

   B) They rotate to create new shapes

   C) They enhance the visual experience

   D) They refract the light

30. What is one of the educational benefits of using a kaleidoscope?

   A) Developing spatial awareness

   B) Enhancing artistic skills

   C) Improving memory retention

   D) Stimulating physical exercise

31. Who can enjoy kaleidoscopes?

   A) Only children

   B) Only adults

   C) Artists and collectors

   D) People of all ages

32. How are modern kaleidoscopes different from traditional ones?

    A) They have rotating mechanisms

    B) They are made of different materials

    C) They produce sound effects

    D) They have built-in cameras

33. What is the main idea of the passage?

    A) The history of kaleidoscopes

    B) The different types of kaleidoscopes

    C) The educational value of kaleidoscopes

    D) The beauty and enjoyment of kaleidoscopes

The Magical Adventures of Toylandia

1. Once upon a time, in a magical world known as Toylandia, a wondrous transformation occurred when the moon bathed the land in its ethereal glow. As the clock struck midnight, toys of all shapes and sizes awakened from their slumber and came to life, eager to embark on enchanting adventures.

2. In this whimsical realm, the streets were lined with sparkling cobblestones and the air was filled with the tinkling sound of laughter. Toy soldiers marched in perfect formation, teddy bears danced in circles, and dolls twirled gracefully in their satin dresses. The toy animals frolicked through meadows of candy-colored flowers, while wind-up cars raced along rainbow-colored tracks.

3. At the heart of Toylandia stood a grand toy castle, where the Toy King and Queen reigned with benevolence. The castle was a sanctuary for lost toys, providing them with love, care, and a sense of belonging. Each toy possessed its own unique magic, granting it the ability to communicate and empathize with children.

4. One night, as the stars shimmered in the sky, a little wooden puppet named Jasper, with eyes as bright as emeralds, yearned for a special purpose beyond his toy box. With a sprinkle of stardust, his wish was granted, and he found himself transported to Toylandia.

5. Jasper's heart fluttered with excitement as he explored the enchanting world. He made friends with a mischievous wind-up monkey named Coco and a wise old teddy bear named Mr. Barnaby. Together, they embarked on thrilling escapades, solving puzzles, and bringing joy to children's lives.

6. In Toylandia, Jasper discovered the true meaning of friendship and the power of imagination. He realized that toys had the remarkable ability to ignite dreams, spark creativity, and provide comfort in times of need. They became the bridge between the real world and the realm of endless possibilities.

7. As dawn approached, the toys returned to their still forms, awaiting the next moonlit adventure. Toylandia was a secret world, hidden from grown-up eyes, where toys could be more than mere playthings. It was a place where they became cherished companions, spreading happiness and magic to children throughout the world.

8. And so, the story of Toylandia continued, with toys coming to life every night, reminding children and adults alike of the enchantment that exists in the simplest of objects and the power of imagination to transform the ordinary into the extraordinary.

34. In which paragraph does the story introduce the magical world of Toylandia?

    A) Paragraph 1

    B) Paragraph 2

    C) Paragraph 3

    D) Paragraph 4

35. Where do the toys in Toylandia go when dawn approaches?

    A) Toylandia Castle

    B) The meadows of candy-colored flowers

    C) Children's homes

    D) Their toy boxes

36. What did Jasper discover about toys in Toylandia?

    A) They could fly

    B) They had the power of invisibility

    C) They could communicate and empathize with children

    D) They could grant wishes

37. Which paragraph describes the Toylandia castle as a sanctuary for lost toys?

    A) Paragraph 1

    B) Paragraph 2

    C) Paragraph 3

    D) Paragraph 4

38. Who were Jasper's friends in Toylandia?

　　A) Coco and Teddy

　　B) Mr. Barnaby and Coco

　　C) Teddy and Mr. Barnaby

　　D) Coco and Jasper

39. What is the main message of the story?

　　A) Toys are just ordinary playthings

　　B) Imagination can transform the ordinary into the extraordinary

　　C) Adults should never enter Toylandia

　　D) Toys should only be played with during the day

40. At the end of the story, what are the toys in Toylandia MOST likely to do?

　　A) Have a tea party with the Toy King and Queen.

　　B) Transform into real-life animals and explore the world.

　　C) Return to their original toy forms and await the next moonlit adventure.

　　D) Build a new toy castle in a different part of Toylandia.

41. What could be an alternative title for the story of Toylandia?

　　A) "The Adventures of Jasper on the flight"

　　B) "A Magical Night in Toylandia"

　　C) "The Enchanted World of Humans"

　　D) "Exploring Toys"

Emily And Grandpa's Enchanting Journey Through Nature

1. Once upon a time, in a small village nestled amidst rolling hills and green meadows, lived a curious little girl named Emily and her wise and loving grandfather, Thomas. They shared a special bond and often embarked on exciting adventures together. One sunny morning, as the birds sang their melodious tunes, Emily skipped into her grandfather's study.

2. "Grandpa, it's such a beautiful day! Can we go for a walk through the country roads today?" Emily asked with sparkling eyes. Grandpa Thomas looked up from his book, his face breaking into a warm smile. "Of course, my dear Emily! I was just thinking the same thing. Let's explore the wonders of nature together."

3. Excitedly, Emily grabbed her grandfather's hand, and they set off on their journey along the winding country roads. The air was crisp, and the scent of wildflowers filled their nostrils. "Look, Grandpa!" Emily pointed to a vibrant butterfly fluttering by. "What kind of butterfly is that?"

4. Grandpa Thomas stopped and observed the delicate creature. "Ah, that's a swallowtail butterfly, Emily. Its wings are like a work of art, painted with bright colors to attract our attention. "Emily's eyes widened with wonder. "It's so beautiful, Grandpa. Do all butterflies have different patterns?"

5. "Indeed they do," Grandpa replied. "Each butterfly species has its own unique pattern. It's like they wear their own special outfit to stand out in the world." As they continued their walk, they passed a babbling brook. Emily knelt down by the water, mesmerized by the tiny fish swimming among the pebbles. "Grandpa, why do fish swim together in groups like that?"

6. Emily asked, her finger tracing the water's surface. "Those are minnows, my dear," Grandpa explained. "Fish often swim in groups, called schools, for protection and to find food more easily. They watch out for each other and stay together." Emily nodded, absorbing the knowledge. "Just like we stay together, Grandpa."

7. Grandpa Thomas smiled, his heart swelling with love for his granddaughter. "Yes, Emily. We are like our own little school, always looking out for one another." They continued their journey, taking in the sights and sounds of nature. They spotted squirrels scampering up trees, birds building nests, and flowers blooming in a riot of colors. As they strolled along a winding path, Emily noticed an old oak tree with gnarled branches. "Grandpa, do you think this tree has a story to tell?" she wondered aloud.

8. Grandpa Thomas leaned against the tree, his hand on Emily's shoulder. "Oh, I'm sure it does, Emily. This old tree has witnessed countless seasons, storms, and generations of creatures passing by. If only it could speak, it would tell us tales of the past." Emily hugged her grandfather tightly. "I love listening to your stories, Grandpa. You always make everything come alive."

9. Grandpa Thomas chuckled, his eyes twinkling with joy. "And I love sharing them with you, my dear Emily. Stories connect us to the wonders of the world, just like our walk through the country roads today. "Hand in hand, Emily and her grandfather continued their walk, their hearts filled with love and the magic of their shared adventures. The country roads became their gateway to endless discoveries, and they treasured each moment spent together in nature's embrace.

42. Where did Emily and her grandfather go for a walk?

   A) City streets

   B) Beach

   C) Country roads

   D) Forest

43. What did Emily find near the babbling brook?

   A) Butterflies

   B) Squirrels

   C) Fish

   D) Birds

44. What is the purpose of the butterflies' colorful wings?

   A) To blend in with their surroundings

   B) To scare away predators

   C) To attract attention

   D) To keep them warm

45. Why do fish swim together in groups?

   A) For mating purposes

   B) To find food more easily

   C) To escape from predators

   D) To sleep together

46. What kind of tree did Emily and her grandfather come across?

   A) Pine tree

   B) Maple tree

   C) Oaktree

   D) Willow tree

47. What do Emily and her grandfather do when they come across the old tree?

    A) They climb it

    B) They sit under its shade

    C) They listen to its stories

    D) They take pictures of it

48. What does the word "mesmerized" mean in the context of the story?

    A) Frightened

    B) Bored

    C) Fascinated

    D) Confused

49. In which sentence is the word "school" used with its primary meaning?

    A) She completed her schooling last year.

    B) The old building had been transformed into a school of art.

    C) She schooled herself in various subjects to broaden her knowledge.

    D) The school of fish moved in perfect synchronization.

50. What would be the most suitable alternative title for Emily's story?

    A) A Walk in the Countryside

    B) Emily and Her Grandfather

    C) Grandpa Thomas

    D) The Curious Little Girl and the Country Roads

Grade 5
ELA Practice Test 2

Grade 5

ELA Practice Test 2

Directions: *Read the passages and answer the questions that follow.*

THE GENERAL AND THE FOX - BY JAMES BALDWIN

There was once a famous Greek general whose name was Aristomenes.

[Aristomenes (pro. ar is tom'e neez)]

He was brave and wise; and his countrymen loved him.

Once, however, in a great battle with the Spartans, his army was beaten and he was taken prisoner.

In those days, people had not learned to be kind to their enemies. In war, they were savage and cruel; for war always makes men so.

The Spartans hated Aristomenes. He had given them a great deal of trouble, and they wished to destroy him.

On a mountain near their city, there was a narrow chasm or hole in the rocks. It was very deep, and there was no way to climb out of it.

The Spartans said to one another, "Let us throw this fellow into the rocky chasm. Then we may be sure that he will never trouble us again."

So a party of soldiers led him up into the mountain and placed him on the edge of the yawning hole in the rocks. "See the place to which we send all our enemies," they said. And they threw him in.

No one knows how he escaped being dashed to pieces. Some of the Greeks said that an eagle caught him in her beak and carried him unharmed to the bottom. But that is not likely.

I think that he must have fallen upon some bushes and vines that grew in some parts of the chasm. At any rate he was not hurt much.

He groped around in the dim light, but could not find any way of escape. The rocky walls surrounded him on every side. There was no place where he could set his foot to climb out.

For three days he lay in his strange prison. He grew weak from hunger and thirst. He expected to die from starvation.

Suddenly he was startled by a noise close by him. Something was moving among the rocks at the bottom of the chasm. He watched quietly, and soon saw a large fox coming towards him.

He lay quite still till the animal was very near. Then he sprang up quickly and seized it by the tail.

The frightened fox scampered away as fast as it could; and Aristomenes followed, clinging to its tail. It ran into a narrow cleft which he had not seen before, and then through a long, dark passage which was barely large enough for a man's body.

Aristomenes held on. At last he saw a ray of light far ahead of him. It was the sunlight streaming in at the entrance to the passage. But soon the way became too narrow for his body to pass through. What should he do? He let go of the fox, and it ran out. Then with great labor he began to widen the passageway. Here the rocks were smaller, and he soon loosened them enough to allow him to squeeze through. In a short time he was free and in the open air.

Some days after this the Spartans heard strange news: "Aristomenes is again at the head of the Greek army." They could not believe it.

1. Which best represents the chasm in the rocks where Aristomenes was thrown?

   A) A deep and narrow rocky abyss

   B) A vast open field

   C) A serene mountain peak

   D) A dense forest

2. What does the word "scampered" mean in the context of the passage?

   A) Moved stealthily and quietly.

   B) Ran quickly and playfully.

   C) Climbed with great effort.

   D) Crawled slowly and cautiously.

3. What happened to the Greek general Aristomenes in a battle with the Spartans?

   A) He was captured and taken prisoner.

   B) He led his army to victory.

   C) He escaped unharmed from the battle.

   D) He was wounded but survived the battle.

4. How did the Spartans plan to deal with Aristomenes after capturing him?

    A) They wanted to negotiate a peace treaty with him.

    B) They admired his bravery and decided to release him.

    C) They intended to throw him into a deep chasm.

    D) They planned to offer him a high-ranking position in their army.

5. How did Aristomenes manage to survive after being thrown into the chasm?

    A) An eagle carried him to safety.

    B) He was rescued by a group of Greeks.

    C) He found a hidden tunnel.

    D) He fell onto bushes and vines.

6. What led Aristomenes to discover a narrow passageway out of the chasm?

    A) A sound of movement among the rocks.

    B) A ray of light shining from above.

    C) A fox that came towards him.

    D) A group of Spartans searching for him.

7. How did Aristomenes eventually escape from the chasm?

    A) By climbing up the rocky walls.

    B) By following the fox through a narrow passage.

    C) By calling for help until someone found him.

    D) By digging a new pathway with his bare hands.

8. Which sentence best states the theme of this story?

    A) The power of perseverance and determination.

    B) The importance of being kind to one's enemies.

    C) The bravery and wisdom of Aristomenes.

    D) The savagery and cruelty of war.

Mrs. Spring Fragrance – BY SUI SIN FAR

1. Mrs. Spring Fragrance came to Seattle without knowing any American words. But after five years, she had learned so many American words that her husband said, "There are no more American words for her learning." Everyone who knew Mrs. Spring Fragrance agreed with Mr. Spring Fragrance.

2. Mr. Spring Fragrance, also known as Sing Yook, was a curio merchant. He was Chinese but had become "Americanized." Mrs. Spring Fragrance was even more "Americanized" than her husband.

3. Their neighbors, the Chin Yuens, lived next door. Mrs. Chin Yuen was older than Mrs. Spring Fragrance, and they had a daughter named Laura, who was eighteen years old. Laura and Mrs. Spring Fragrance were good friends. Laura had an American name, and she was called Laura by almost everyone, including her parents and Chinese friends. Laura had a boyfriend named Kai Tzu. Kai Tzu was born in America and was a talented baseball player. He was known as one of the best pitchers on the Coast. He could also sing a beautiful song called "Drink to me only with thine eyes," while Laura played the piano.

4. Only Mrs. Spring Fragrance knew that Kai Tzu and Laura loved each other. The reason for this was that Laura's parents had arranged for her to marry the eldest son of a Chinese Government school-teacher in San Francisco. They followed many Chinese customs and traditions. The time for Laura's betrothal was approaching.

5. One day, Laura was with Mrs. Spring Fragrance, feeling sad. Mrs. Spring Fragrance tried to cheer her up by talking about her walk that day. She described the beautiful daffodils in the green grass and the fragrance of the wallflower. Laura burst into tears because it was a walk she and Kai Tzu used to enjoy together.

6. Mrs. Spring Fragrance comforted Laura and told her about a beautiful American poem by a noble American named Frost. The poem said, " The woods are lovely, dark and deep, But I have promises to keep, And miles to go before I sleep, And miles to go before I sleep." The name of the poem was *Stopping by the woods on a snowy evening*. Mrs. Spring Fragrance didn't know that her husband was listening to their conversation from the veranda. He repeated the lines of the poem, but he didn't want to hear any more of their secret talk, so he walked to the other side of the house.

7. In his pocket, Mr. Spring Fragrance found a little box. Inside was a jadestone pendant that he had bought for Mrs. Spring Fragrance as a gift on their fifth wedding anniversary. He put the box back in his pocket.

8. Suddenly, a young man came out of the house next door. Mr. Spring Fragrance greeted him, and they started talking. Mr. Spring Fragrance asked the young man to explain the meaning of two lines from the American verse he had heard. The young man, who was a student at the University of Washington, thought he knew everything and was happy to explain.

9. The lines were, "'Tis better to have loved and lost, than never to have loved at all." The young man said it meant that it was good to love someone even if we couldn't be with them or if we lost them. He believed that we need experience to understand the truth of this teaching.

10. Mr. Spring Fragrance didn't agree with the young man's explanation. He said there was no truth in it. He believed it was better to have something we don't love than to love something we don't have.

11. As the evening went on, Mr. Spring Fragrance and the young man continued their discussion, each having their own opinion about love and loss.

9. According to the passage, what is Mrs. Spring Fragrance's opinion of the American language?

    A) She finds it challenging to learn.

    B) She believes it is unnecessary to learn.

    C) She considers it beautiful and important.

    D) She thinks it is inferior to the Chinese language.

10. What American poem did Mrs. Spring Fragrance mention?

    A) "Drink to me only with thine eyes"

    B) "Stopping by the woods"

    C) "To be, or not to be"

    D) "The Raven"

11. In paragraph 2, the word "Americanized" most likely means:

    A) Familiar with American customs and culture

    B) Born and raised in America

    C) Having American ancestry

    D) Traveling frequently to America

12. What did Mr. Spring Fragrance mean when he said, "There are no more American words for her learning"?

    A) Mrs. Spring Fragrance was still learning American words

    B) Mrs. Spring Fragrance couldn't learn any more American words

    C) Mrs. Spring Fragrance had forgotten the American words she had learned

    D) Mrs. Spring Fragrance had learned all the American words

13. What was Kai Tzu known for?

A) Singing American songs

B) Playing the piano

C) Being a talented baseball player

D) Writing poetry

14. What did Mrs. Spring Fragrance try to cheer Laura up with?

A) Talking about a beautiful walk

B) Giving her a gift

C) Playing the piano

D) Taking her to a baseball game

15. How did Mr. Spring Fragrance respond to the American poem?

A) He agreed with the message of the poem

B) He disagreed with the message of the poem

C) He didn't understand the meaning of the poem

D) He repeated the lines of the poem

16. What did Mr. Spring Fragrance find in his pocket?

A) A jadestone pendant

B) A poem, written by Tennyson

C) A box of chocolates

D) Laura's love letter

17. The suffix in the word *suddenly* is

A) -enly

B) -nly

C) -ly

D) -y

The Dragon Tamers - E. Nesbit

There was once an old, old castle—it was so old that its walls and towers and turrets and gateways and arches had crumbled to ruins, and of all its old splendor there were only two little rooms left; and it was here that John the blacksmith had set up his forge.

He was too poor to live in a proper house, and no one asked any rent for the rooms in the ruin, because all the lords of the castle were dead and gone this many a year. So there John blew his bellows and hammered his iron and did all the work which came his way. This was not much, because most of the trade went to the mayor of the town, who was also a blacksmith in quite a large way of business, and had his huge forge facing the square of the town, and had twelve apprentices, all hammering like a nest of woodpeckers, and twelve journeymen to order the apprentices about, and a patent forge and a self-acting hammer and electric bellows, and all things handsome about him. So of course the townspeople, whenever they wanted a horse shod or a shaft mended, went to the mayor.

John the blacksmith struggled on as best he could, with a few odd jobs from travelers and strangers who did not know what a superior forge the mayor's was. The two rooms were warm and weather-tight, but not very large; so the blacksmith got into the way of keeping his old iron, his odds and ends, his fagots, and his two pence worth of coal in the great dungeon down under the castle.

It was a very fine dungeon indeed, with a handsome vaulted roof and big iron rings whose staples were built into the wall, very strong and convenient for tying captives to, and at one end was a broken flight of wide steps leading down no one knew where. Even the lords of the castle in the good old times had never known where those steps led to, but every now and then they would kick a prisoner down the steps in their lighthearted, hopeful way, and sure enough, the prisoners never came back. The blacksmith had never dared to go beyond the seventh step, and no more have I—so I know no more than he did what was at the bottom of those stairs.

John, the blacksmith, had a wife and a little baby. When his wife was not doing the housework, she used to nurse the baby and cry, remembering the happy days when she lived with her father, who kept seventeen cows and lived in the country, and when John used to come courting her in the summer evenings, as smart, with a posy in his buttonhole. And now John's hair was getting gray, and there was hardly ever enough to eat.

As for the baby, it cried a good deal at odd times; but at night, when its mother had settled down to sleep, it would always begin to cry, quite as a matter of course, so that she hardly got any rest at all. This made her very tired.

The baby could make up for its bad nights during the day if it liked, but the poor mother couldn't. So whenever she had nothing to do she used to sit and cry, because she was tired out with work and worry.

18. Where did John the blacksmith set up his forge?

    A) In a proper house   B) In the mayor's large forge

    C) In a ruinous castle   D) In the town square

19. Why did John the blacksmith keep his old iron and other materials in the dungeon?

    A) Because it was warm and weather-tight

    B) Because it had a vaulted roof

    C) Because it was convenient for tying captives

    D) Because it was the only available storage space

20. What did the lords of the castle do to prisoners?

    A) Sent them to work in the blacksmith's forge

    B) Released them after a short time

    C) Sent them down the broken flight of steps

    D) Gave them a fair trial and punishment

21. Why did John the blacksmith's wife cry?

    A) Because she missed her father's cows

    B) Because John's hair was getting gray

    C) Because she was tired from taking care of the baby

    D) Because they did not have enough to eat

22. What is one of the major differences between John the blacksmith's forge and the mayor's forge in the story?

    A) The mayor's forge is located in a proper house.

    B) The mayor's forge has a self-acting hammer and electric bellows.

    C) The mayor's forge is situated in the countryside.

    D) The mayor's forge is operated by twelve apprentices.

23. Read the dictionary entry:

> **Ruin [roo-ins]**
>
> 1. to reduce to a fallen, wrecked, or decayed condition; devastate.
>
> 2. to bring (a person, company, etc.) to financial destruction; bankrupt.
>
> 3. the remains of a building, city, etc.
>
> 4. to come to downfall or destruction.

Which meaning of the word *ruins* is used in this passage?

A) 1   B) 2

C) 3   D) 4

24. Why did most of the trade go to the mayor of the town?

A) Because the townspeople did not know about John's forge

B) Because the mayor's apprentices were more skilled

C) Because the mayor had lower prices than John the blacksmith

D) Because the mayor had a large forge with advanced equipment

25. What did John the blacksmith keep in the dungeon?

A) His family's belongings

B) His odds and ends and coal

C) His tools and equipment

D) His customers' orders

26. Based on the description of the ruinous castle, which phrase represents the two little rooms where John the blacksmith set up his forge?

A) A grand castle with intact walls and towers

B) A dilapidated castle with ruins and two small rooms

C) A bustling town square with a large forge

D) A modern blacksmith's workshop with advanced equipment

THE YOUNG KING – OSCAR WILDE

TO

MARGARET LADY BROOKE

[THE RANEE OF SARAWAK]

It was the night before the day fixed for his coronation, and the young King was sitting alone in his beautiful chamber. His courtiers had all taken their leave of him, bowing their heads to the ground, according to the ceremonious usage of the day, and had retired to the Great Hall of the Palace, to receive a few last lessons from the Professor of Etiquette; there being some of them who had still quite natural manners, which in a courtier is, I need hardly say, a very grave offence.

The lad—for he was only a lad, being but sixteen years of age—was not sorry at their departure, and had flung himself back with a deep sigh of relief on the soft cushions of his embroidered couch, lying there, wild-eyed and open-mouthed, like a brown woodland Faun, or some young animal of the forest newly snared by the hunters.

And, indeed, it was the hunters who had found him, coming upon him almost by chance as, bare-limbed and pipe in hand, he was following the flock of the poor goatherd who had brought him up, and whose son he had always fancied himself to be. The child of the old King's only daughter by a secret marriage with one much beneath her in station—a stranger, some said, who, by the wonderful magic of his lute-playing, had made the young Princess love him—he had been, when but a week old, stolen away from his mother's side, as she slept, and given into the charge of a common peasant and his wife, who were without children of their own, and lived in a remote part of the forest, more than a day's ride from the town.

Grief, or the plague, as the court physician stated, or, as some suggested, a swift Italian poison administered in a cup of spiced wine, slew, within an hour of her wakening, the white girl who had given him birth, and as the trusty messenger who bore the child across his saddle-bow stooped from his weary horse and knocked at the rude door of the goatherd's hut, the body of the Princess was being lowered into an open grave that had been dug in a deserted churchyard, beyond the city gates, a grave where it was said that another body was also lying, that of a young man of marvelous and foreign beauty, whose hands were tied behind him with a knotted cord, and whose breast was stabbed with many red wounds.

Grade 5

ELA Practice Test 2

Such, at least, was the story that men whispered to each other. Certain it was that the old King, when on his deathbed, whether moved by remorse for his great sin, or merely desiring that the kingdom should not pass away from his line, had had the lad sent for, and, in the presence of the Council, had acknowledged him as his heir.

27. Where did the courtiers go after taking their leave of the young King?

    A) The Great Hall of the Palace   B) The Chamber of Secrets

    C) The Royal Gardens   D) The Professor's Quarters

28. How did the young King feel when the courtiers left?

    A) Relieved   B) Disappointed

    C) Angry   D) Indifferent

29. According to the passage, what were the possible reasons for the young King's mother's death?

    A) Grief or the plague

    B) Swift Italian poison

    C) Both A) and B)

    D) The text does not provide a clear reason

30. What details about the young King's mother's burial suggest a mysterious and potentially sinister backstory?

    A) She was buried in a deserted churchyard.

    B) Another body, that of a young man with stab wounds, was buried alongside her.

    C) Her grave was dug beyond the city gates.

    D) All of the above.

31. What is the meaning of the word 'knocked' as used in the sentence

   "his weary horse and knocked at the rude door of the goatherd's hut"?

   A) Tapped lightly

   B) Banged forcefully

   C) Scratched gently

   D) Pushed open

32. Read the dictionary entry:

> **grave** [greyv]
>
> 1. A hole dug in the ground for burying a dead body.
>
> 2. Serious and solemn in manner or appearance.
>
> 3. A mark or spot made by pressure or rubbing.
>
> 4. A slow and solemn musical composition.

   Which meaning of the word *grave* is used in paragraph 1?

   A) 1

   B) 2

   C) 3

   D) 4

33. What is the young King's relationship to the old King?

   A) He is the old King's son

   B) He is the old King's nephew

   C) He is the old King's grandson

   D) The text does not specify their exact relationship

34. How did the old King acknowledge the young King as his heir?

  A) In a public proclamation

  B) In a private letter

  C) In the presence of the Council

  D) The text does not mention how it was done

35. What event led to the old King's decision to make the young King his heir?

  A) The young King's exceptional musical talent

  B) The old King's remorse for a past sin

  C) The young King's popularity among the people

  D) The Council's recommendation

READIG COMPREHENSION

1. Once upon a time, in the early 19th century, in the picturesque town of Nottinghamshire, England, two young boys named William and Thomas found themselves embroiled in an unexpected adventure. It was a time of economic hardship, and the region was plagued by a notorious band of robbers who terrorized the local villagers. Unbeknownst to William and Thomas, fate had chosen them to become unlikely heroes.

2. William, a quick-witted and resourceful lad, hailed from a modest farming family. His friend Thomas, on the other hand, was the son of a skilled blacksmith, known for his strength and craftsmanship. Together, the two boys shared a deep bond of friendship and a thirst for adventure.

3. One sunny afternoon, as they ventured into Sherwood Forest to explore, William and Thomas stumbled upon a hidden cave. Intrigued by its mysterious aura, they cautiously entered, only to discover that it served as the secret hideout for the band of robbers who had been plaguing their town.

4. Filled with a sense of duty and a desire to protect their community, the boys hatched a plan. They observed the robbers' activities, learning their routines and the layout of the cave. Armed with this knowledge, they decided to gather evidence against the criminals and expose their crimes.

5. Over the following weeks, William and Thomas worked tirelessly to gather information, meticulously documenting the robbers' stolen treasures and their plans for future heists. They kept their activities a secret, not wanting to endanger themselves or their families.

6. When they felt they had gathered enough evidence, the boys devised a daring plan. They sought the aid of the local constable, a wise and experienced man named Constable Albert, who had been tirelessly trying to apprehend the band of robbers. Initially skeptical of their abilities, the constable recognized the bravery and determination in their eyes and agreed to support their endeavor.

7. Under the cover of darkness, the trio infiltrated the cave with the assistance of a small group of trusted villagers. Armed with stealth and bravery, they crept through the shadows, carefully avoiding the robbers' watchful eyes. As they closed in on the criminals, the boys' hearts pounded with a mixture of fear and excitement.

8. Suddenly, their cover was blown as one of the robbers spotted them. Panic ensued as the outlaws sprang into action, attempting to escape with their ill-gotten gains. But William and Thomas, fueled by their unwavering determination, courageously confronted the robbers.

9. The ensuing battle was fierce and chaotic. With Constable Albert and the villagers providing backup, the boys displayed remarkable wit and agility, outsmarting the robbers at every turn. Though outnumbered and facing experienced criminals, William and Thomas fought valiantly, using their knowledge of the cave's layout to their advantage. Finally, the local authorities arrived, having been alerted by the commotion. With their combined efforts, they apprehended the remaining robbers and put an end to their reign of terror.

10. News of William and Thomas's bravery spread quickly throughout Nottinghamshire, and the townsfolk hailed them as heroes. They were celebrated for their ingenuity, resilience, and selflessness. The local authorities presented the boys with commendations, and their families beamed with pride.

11. The events of that day forever changed the lives of William and Thomas. Their courage and determination became a legendary tale, inspiring future generations to stand up against injustice. As they grew older, the boys continued to be known for their noble deeds, becoming respected members of the community.

12. The tale of two young boys who stopped a band of robbers became a cherished part of Nottinghamshire's history, reminding everyone that bravery knows no age and that even the smallest among us can make a profound difference.

36. Which of the following would be a suitable title for the thrilling historical adventure where two boys stop a band of robbers in Nottinghamshire?

    A) Shadows of Justice: The Heroic Journey of William and Thomas

    B) Robbers' Defeat: The Unlikely Triumph of Two Young Boys

    C) Adventures in Nottinghamshire: The Courageous Exploits of William and Thomas

    D) The Boys Who Stopped the Band: A Tale of Bravery in Nottinghamshire

37. Which of the following phrases is the most suitable synonym for "noble deeds" (paragraph 11)?

    A) Courageous acts

    B) Admirable actions

    C) Heroic accomplishments

    D) Valiant endeavors

38. What is the main reason for paragraph 1?

    A) To tell us about the time and place of the story.

    B) To explain the problems faced by the town.

    C) To introduce the main characters, William and Thomas.

    D) To show how good friends William and Thomas are.

39. Where did William and Thomas find the hidden cave?

    A) Sherwood Forest

    B) Nottinghamshire village

    C) William's farm

    D) Constable Albert's house

40. Who assisted William and Thomas in their mission to stop the robbers?

    A) The local authorities

    B) The villagers

    C) The robbers' gang

    D) Constable Albert's family

41. How did the townsfolk react to William and Thomas's actions?

    A) They criticized them

    B) They ignored them

    C) They hailed them as heroes

    D) They doubted their bravery

42. Read this sentence.

Filled with a sense of duty and a desire to protect their community, the boys hatched a plan. They observed the robbers' activities, learning their routines and the **layout** *of the cave.*

What does the word *layout* mean as used in the passage?

    A) The arrangement or organization of objects, elements, or information in a particular space or design.

    B) A plot of land used for agricultural purposes.

    C) The process of drawing or designing the outline or structure of something.

    D) A plan or blueprint for the construction of a building or infrastructure.

Preserving the Jewels of the Sea: Combating the Depletion of Coral Reefs

1. Coral reefs are incredibly diverse and vibrant ecosystems that are often referred to as the "rainforests of the sea." These underwater structures, built by tiny coral polyps, provide a home to a multitude of marine species and play a crucial role in maintaining the health of our oceans. However, in recent years, coral reefs have been facing a severe threat—depletion.

2. The depletion of coral reefs is primarily attributed to a combination of human activities and environmental factors. One of the most significant contributors to reef depletion is climate change. Rising sea temperatures, caused by global warming, result in coral bleaching—a phenomenon in which corals expel the symbiotic algae living within their tissues, causing them to turn white and become vulnerable to disease. The frequency and severity of coral bleaching events have increased dramatically, leaving vast stretches of once vibrant reefs devoid of life.

3. Another human-induced factor contributing to coral reef depletion is overfishing and destructive fishing practices. Unsustainable fishing practices, such as blast fishing and the use of cyanide, not only harm coral colonies directly but also disrupt the delicate balance of the reef ecosystem. Removing key fish species from the food chain can lead to imbalances in population and the degradation of coral reef health.

4. Pollution, specifically from land-based sources, also poses a significant threat to coral reefs. Runoff from agricultural activities, sewage discharge, and excessive use of fertilizers introduce high levels of sediment, nutrients, and chemical pollutants into coastal waters. These pollutants can smother corals, inhibit their growth, and trigger harmful algae blooms, further stressing the reef ecosystem.

5. In addition to these human activities, natural phenomena such as storms, hurricanes, and ocean acidification also impact coral reefs. Violent storms can physically damage coral structures, while ocean acidification, caused by the absorption of excess carbon dioxide from the atmosphere, weakens coral skeletons, making them more susceptible to erosion and breakdown.

6. The depletion of coral reefs has far-reaching consequences for both the marine environment and human populations. Coral reefs provide essential ecosystem services, such as coastal protection from storms, shoreline stabilization, and nurseries for numerous fish species. They also support local economies through tourism, recreational activities, and fishing industries. The loss of coral reefs not only disrupts the delicate balance of marine life but also negatively impacts the livelihoods of millions of people who depend on these ecosystems for their sustenance and income.

7. Efforts to reduce the depletion of coral reefs are crucial for their survival and restoration. Conservation initiatives focus on reducing greenhouse gas emissions to combat climate change, implementing sustainable fishing practices, and improving water quality through better management of coastal activities. Coral restoration projects, such as coral nurseries and artificial reef structures, are also being undertaken to rebuild damaged reefs and promote their recovery.

8. In conclusion, the depletion of coral reefs is an urgent issue. It is imperative that we recognize the value of these fragile ecosystems and take action to protect and restore them. By addressing the root causes of reef depletion and implementing sustainable practices, we can ensure the preservation of these remarkable underwater habitats for future generations to enjoy and benefit from.

43. According to paragraph 2, what is one significant factor contributing to the depletion of coral reefs?

    A) Overfishing and destructive fishing practices

    B) Rising sea temperatures and coral bleaching

    C) Pollution from land-based sources

    D) Storms and hurricanes

44. What is mentioned as an outcome of unsustainable fishing practices?

    A) Coral bleaching

    B) Coastal protection from storms

    C) Imbalances in the population

    D) Sediment and chemical pollutants

45. What are some examples of land-based sources of pollution affecting coral reefs?

    A) Rising sea temperatures and coral bleaching

    B) Violent storms and hurricanes

    C) Runoff from agricultural activities and sewage discharge

    D) Coral nurseries and artificial reef structures

46. What are some ecosystem services provided by coral reefs, as mentioned in paragraph 6?

    A) Coastal protection from storms and shoreline stabilization

    B) Rising sea temperatures and coral bleaching

    C) Sustainable fishing practices and water quality improvement

    D) Tourism, recreational activities, and fishing industries

47. What are some conservation initiatives mentioned to reduce the depletion of coral reefs?

    A) Reducing greenhouse gas emissions and improving water quality

    B) Overfishing and destructive fishing practices

    C) Violent storms and hurricanes

    D) Coral bleaching and ocean acidification

48. What is the main message of the passage, as stated in the concluding paragraph (paragraph 8)?

    A) Coral reefs are vibrant ecosystems built by coral polyps.

    B) Rising sea temperatures and overfishing are depleting coral reefs.

    C) Efforts to protect and restore coral reefs are crucial.

    D) Coral reefs provide ecosystem services and support local economies.

49. Which feature of the below indicates a depleted coral reef?

    A) Colorful and healthy coral colonies

    B) School of vibrant fish swimming around the corals

    C) Bleached and white coral colonies

    D) Various sizes and shapes of coral structures

50. Which definition best describes the use of "nursery" mentioned in paragraph 6 of the passage?

    A) A room or area in a home where young children are cared for.

    B) A place where young plants and trees are grown and nurtured.

    C) A medical facility specializing in the care of newborns.

    D) A school or institution for the education of young children.

Grade 5 ELA Practice Test 3

Directions: *Read the passages and answer the questions that follow.*

JO'S JOURNAL

NEW YORK, November.

DEAR MARMEE AND BETH —

"I'm going to write you a regular volume, for I've got heaps to tell, though I'm not a fine young lady travelling on the continent. When I lost sight of father's dear old face, I felt a trifle blue, and might have shed a briny drop or two, if an Irish lady with four small children, all crying more or less, hadn't diverted my mind; for I amused myself by dropping gingerbread nuts over the seat every time they opened their mouths to roar.

"Soon the sun came out, and taking it as a good omen, I cleared up likewise, and enjoyed my journey with all my heart.

"Mrs. Kirke welcomed me so kindly I felt at home at once, even in that big house full of strangers. She gave me a funny little sky-parlor—all she had; but there is a stove in it, and a nice table in a sunny window, so I can sit here and write whenever I like. A fine view and a church-tower opposite atone for the many stairs, and I took a fancy to my den on the spot. The nursery, where I am to teach and sew, is a pleasant room next Mrs. Kirke's private parlor, and the two little girls are pretty children, —rather spoilt, I fancy, but they took to me after telling them 'The Seven Bad Pigs;' and I've no doubt I shall make a model governess.

"I am to have my meals with the children, if I prefer it to the great table, and for the present I do, for I *am* bashful, though no one will believe it.

"'Now, my dear, make yourself at home,' said Mrs. K. in her motherly way; 'I'm on the drive from morning to night, as you may suppose with such a family; but a great anxiety will be off my mind if I know the children are safe with you. My rooms are always open to you, and your own shall be as comfortable as I can make it. There are some pleasant people in the house if you feel sociable, and your evenings are always free. Come to me if anything goes wrong, and be as happy as you can. There's the tea-bell; I must run and change my cap;' and off she bustled, leaving me to settle myself in my new nest.

"As I went downstairs, soon after, I saw something I liked. The flights are very long in this tall house, and as I stood waiting at the head of the third one for a little servant girl to lumber up, I saw a gentleman come along behind her, take the heavy hod of coal out of her hand, carry it all the way up, put it down at a door near by, and walk away, saying, with a kind nod and a foreign accent,—

"'It goes better so. The little back is too young to haf such heaviness.'

"Wasn't it good of him? I like such things, for, as father says, **trifles show character**. When I mentioned it to Mrs. K., that evening, she laughed, and said, —

"'That must have been Professor Bhaer; he's always doing things of that sort.'

"Mrs. K. told me he was from Berlin; very learned and good, but poor as a church-mouse, and gives lessons to support himself and two little orphan nephews whom he is educating here, according to the wishes of his sister, who married an American. Not a very romantic story, but it interested me; and I was glad to hear that

Mrs. K. lends him her parlor for some of his scholars. There is a glass door between it and the nursery, and I mean to peep at him, and then I'll tell you how he looks. He's almost forty, so it's no harm, Marmee.

"After tea and a go-to-bed romp with the little girls, I attacked the big work-basket, and had a quiet evening chatting with my new friend. I shall keep a journal-letter, and send it once a week; so good-night, and more to-morrow."

1. **Where is the narrator writing from?**
   A. New York
   B. Berlin
   C. Ireland
   D. Chicago

2. **What does the glass door separate?**
   A. The living room and the dining room
   B. The parlour and the nursery
   C. The study and the bedroom
   D. The parlour and the kitchen

3. **Why does Professor Bhaer give lessons?**
   A. To support himself and his orphan nephews
   B. To learn new things
   C. To earn his living as he was as poor as a door-mouse
   D. To teach his orphan nephews

4. **Which of the following is not a meaning of *atone*:**

   1. to do something to make up for a wrong that has been done
   2. to make amends
   3. to reconcile
   4. along with

   A. 1
   B. 2
   C. 3
   D. 4

5. **Which of the following is not true about Jo's stay at the house?**
   A. She was given a funny little sky-parlour
   B. She was supposed to sew and teach in the nursery which was just above Mrs. Kirke's private parlour
   C. Her room had a little stove and a table where she could write whenever she pleased
   D. The children were pampered and it wasn't until she told them. The Seven Bad pigs that they cherished her.

6. **Mrs. K, asks her to make herself at home by -**

   I. Her room is always open for Jo

   II. She made sure that Jo's room was as comfortable as she could make it

   III. She would be happy to make her a cup of tea whenever Jo wanted to talk

   IV. If she wanted to socialize, there were a lot of pleasant people in the house

   A. I, II, III
   B. II, III, IV
   C. I, II, IV
   D. I, III, IV

7. **In the phrase "trifles show character" what is the meaning of trifle?**
   A. to talk in a jesting or mocking manner or with intent to delude or mislead
   B. to handle something idly
   C. a dessert typically consisting of plain or sponge cake often soaked with wine or spirits (such as brandy or rum) and topped with layers of preserves, custard, and cream
   D. something of little value, substance, or importance

8. **This text is in the form of a -**
   A. Diary entry
   B. Postcard
   C. Journal letter
   D. E-mail

"MY HOUSE IS HAUNTED" - Heidi
By Johanna Spyri

For some days past Miss Rottermeyer had gone about rather silently and as if lost in thought. As twilight fell, and she passed from room to room, or along the long corridors, she was seen to look cautiously behind her, and into the dark corners, as if she thought someone was coming up silently behind her and might unexpectedly give her dress a pull. Nor would she now go alone into some parts of the house. If she visited the upper floor where the grand guest-chambers were, or had to go down into the large drawing room, where every footstep echoed, she called Tinette to accompany her.

For something very strange and mysterious was going on in Mr. Sesemann's house. Every morning, when the servants went downstairs, they found the front door wide open, although nobody could be seen far or near to account for it. During the first few days that this happened every room and corner was searched in great alarm, to see if anything had been stolen, for the general idea was that a thief had been hiding in the house and had gone off in the night with the stolen goods; but not a thing in the house had been touched, everything was safe in its place. The door was doubly locked at night, and for further security the wooden bar was fastened across it; but it was no good—next morning the door again stood open. At last, after a great deal of persuasion from Miss Rottermeyer, Sebastian and John plucked up courage and agreed to sit up one night to watch and see what would happen. Miss Rottermeyer hunted up several weapons belonging to the master, and gave these and a bottle of brandy to them so that their courage might not faint if it came to a fight.

On the appointed night the two sat down and began at once to take some of the strengthening cordial, which at first made them very talkative and then very sleepy, so that they leant back in their seats and became silent. As midnight struck, Sebastian roused himself and called to his companion, who, however, was not easy to wake, and kept rolling his head first to one side and then the other and continuing to sleep. Sebastian began to listen more attentively, for he was wide awake now. He did not feel inclined to go to sleep again, for the stillness was ghostly to him, and he was afraid now to raise his voice to rouse John, so he shook him gently to make him stir. At last, as one struck, John woke up, and came back to the consciousness of why he was sitting in a chair instead of lying in his bed. He got up with a great show of courage and said, "Come, Sebastian, we must go out in the hall and see what is going on; you need not be afraid, just follow me."

Whereupon he opened the door wide and stepped into the hall. Just as he did so a sudden gust of air blew through the open front door and put out the light which John held in his hand. He started back, almost overturning Sebastian, whom he clutched and pulled back into the room, and then shutting the door quickly he turned the key as far as he could make it go. Then he pulled out his matches and lighted his candle again. Sebastian, in the suddenness of the affair, did not know exactly what had happened, for he had not seen the open front door or felt the breeze behind John's broad figure. But now, as he saw the latter in the light, he gave a cry of alarm, for John was trembling all over and was as white as a ghost. "What's the matter? What did you see outside?" asked Sebastian sympathetically.

"The door partly open," gasped John, "and a white figure standing at the top of the steps—there it stood, and then all in a minute it disappeared."

Sebastian felt his blood run cold. The two sat down close to one another and did not dare move again till the morning broke and the streets began to be alive again. Then they left the room together, shut the front door, and went upstairs to tell Miss Rottermeyer of their experience. They had no sooner given her details of the night's experience than she sat down and wrote to Mr. Sesemann, who had never received such a letter before in his life. She could hardly write, she told him, for her fingers were stiff with fear, and Mr. Sesemann must please arrange to come back at once, for dreadful and unaccountable things were taking place at home. Then she entered into particulars of all that had happened, of how the door was found standing open every morning.

Mr. Sesemann answered that it was quite impossible for him to arrange to leave his business and return home at once.

Miss Rottermeyer, however, was determined not to pass any more days in a state of fear, and she knew the right course to pursue. She had as yet said nothing to the children of the ghostly apparitions, for she knew if she did that the children would not remain alone for a single moment, and that might entail discomfort for herself. But now she walked straight off into the study, and there in a low, mysterious voice told the two children everything that had taken place. Clara immediately screamed out that she could not remain another minute alone, her father must come home.

So Miss Rottermeyer wrote another letter to Mr. Sesemann, stating that these unaccountable things that were going on in the house had so affected his daughter's **delicate constitution** that the worst consequences might be expected. Epileptic fits and St. Vitus's dance often came on suddenly in cases like this, and Clara was liable to be attacked by either if the cause of the general alarm was not removed.

The letter was successful, and two days later Mr. Sesemann arrived home.

Clara greeted him with a cry of joy, and seeing her so lively and apparently as well as ever, his face cleared, and the frown of anxiety passed gradually away from it as he heard from his daughter's own lips that she had nothing the matter with her, and moreover was so delighted to see him that she was quite glad about the ghost, as it was the cause of bringing him home again.

Answer the below questions

9. Why did Miss Rottermeyer call Tinette to accompany her in certain areas of the house?
- A. She needed help carrying something
- B. She was afraid of the dark
- C. She believed someone might be following her
- D. She wanted a companion for conversation

10. What did the servants find every morning when they went downstairs?
- A. Broken windows
- B. Missing items from the house
- C. A thief hiding in the house
- D. The front door wide open

11. What was the general idea as to why the front door was open every morning?
    A. The servants forgot to lock it properly
    B. A thief had been hiding in the house and stolen goods
    C. The door was malfunctioning
    D. The wind had blown it open

12. What did Sebastian and John do to prepare for their night of watching?
    A. Drank brandy and gathered weapons
    B. Called the police for assistance
    C. Brought blankets and pillows
    D. Turned off all the lights in the house

13. Why did Sebastian give a cry of alarm when he saw John in the light?
    A. John had fallen asleep in his chair
    B. John had dropped the weapon he was holding
    C. John had seen the ghostly apparition
    D. John was trembling all over and as white as a ghost

14. Why did Clara initially insist that her father come home?
    A. Because she was experiencing health issues
    B. Because she could not bear being alone anymore
    C. Because she missed him and wanted to see him
    D. Because she thought he could solve the mystery

15. On receiving the 2nd letter -
    A. He sent additional weapons and brandy for protection
    B. He arranged to come home two days later
    C. He ignored the letter and continued with his business
    D. He hired a detective to investigate the ghostly happenings

16. What does the word '**constitution**' mean as it is used in this sentence?

> So Miss Rottermeyer wrote another letter to Mr. Sesemann, stating that these unaccountable things that were going on in the house had so affected his daughter's delicate **constitution** that the worst consequences might be expected.

   A. a written instrument embodying the rules of a political or social organization
   B. the physical makeup of the individual especially with respect to the health, strength, and appearance of the body
   C. an established law or custom
   D. the act of establishing, making, or setting up

THE FIRST VOYAGE OF SINDBAD THE SAILOR

1. My father was a rich merchant of good fame. He left me a large estate, which I wasted in riotous living. I quickly saw my error, especially in misspending my time, which is of all things the most valuable. I remembered the saying of the great Solomon, which I had often heard from my father, "A good name is better than precious ointment;" and again, "Wisdom is good with an inheritance." I resolved to walk in my father's ways, and embarked with some merchants on board a ship we had fitted out together.

2. We steered our course towards the Indies. At first, I was troubled with seasickness, but speedily regained my health. In our voyage, we touched several islands, where we sold or exchanged our goods. One day, whilst under sail, we were becalmed near a small island rising but little above the level of the water and resembling a green meadow. The captain permitted such persons as were so **inclined** to land; of this number I was one. But whilst we were eating and drinking, and resting from the fatigue of the sea, the island all of a sudden trembled and shook us terribly.

3. The trembling of the island was soon noticed on board the ship, and we were called to reëmbark quickly, or we should all be lost; for what we took to be an island proved to be the back of a sea monster. The **nimblest** got into the **sloop**; others betook themselves to swimming; as for me, I was still upon the island when it sank into the sea, and I had only time to catch hold of a piece of wood that we brought from the ship to make a fire. Meanwhile the captain, having taken the others on board, resolved to make the most of the favoring gale that had just risen, and sailed away.

4. Thus was I left to the mercy of the waves for the rest of the day and the night that followed. By this time I found my strength gone, and was despairing of my life when happily a wave threw me against an island. The bank was high and rugged, but some roots of trees helped me to get up. When the sun arose, I was very feeble but managed to find some herbs that were fit to eat and a spring of good water. Thus refreshed, I advanced farther into the island and reached a fine plain, where I saw some horses feeding. As I went towards them, I heard the voice of a man who appeared and asked me who I was. When I had told him my adventure, he led me by the hand into a cave, where there were several other people, no less amazed to see me than I was to see them.

5. I partook of some food which they gave me and then learned that they were grooms belonging to the sovereign of the island, where they brought the king's horses every year for pasturage. They were to return home on the morrow, and had I been one day later I must have perished, because the inhabited part of the island was far off, and I could never have reached it without a guide.

6. The next morning they took me to the capital of the island and presented me to the sovereign. When at his request I told him of my misfortune, he was much concerned, and gave orders that I should want for nothing; and his commands were carefully fulfilled.

7. As a merchant I met with many men of my own profession, and sought news from Bagdad, and the opportunity to return; for the capital of the island has a fine harbor, where ships arrive daily from many quarters of the world. I took delight also in hearing the talk of learned Indians, and withal paid my court to the sovereign, and met with the governors and petty kings that were subject to him, telling and learning much.

8. There belongs to this king an island named Cassel, where the mariners said that every night the noise of drums might be heard. This wonderful place I visited, and on the way thither saw fishes of one hundred and two hundred cubits in length, that occasion more fear than hurt; for they are so timid that they will fly upon the rattling of two sticks or boards. I saw likewise other fishes, about a cubit in length, that had heads like owls.

9. One day, as I was at the port after this visit, the ship arrived in which I had embarked at Bussorah. I knew the captain at once, and went and asked him for my bales. "I am Sindbad," said I, "and those bales marked with his name are mine."

10. "Heavens!" he exclaimed, "whom can we trust in these times? I saw Sindbad perish with my own eyes, and now you tell this tale to possess yourself of what does not belong to you."

11. But at length he was persuaded that I was no cheat, for there came people from his ship who knew me, and expressed much joy at seeing me alive. "Heaven be praised," said he at last, "for your happy escape! There are your goods; take and do with them as you please." What was of greatest worth in them I presented to the sovereign, who was much pleased to hear of my good fortune, and gave me in return a gift of still greater value. Then I took leave of him, and went aboard the same ship after I had exchanged my goods for products of that country. I carried with me wood of aloes, sandals, camphire, nutmegs, cloves, pepper, and ginger. We passed by several islands, and at last arrived at Bussorah, whence I came to this city with great wealth.

12. Here Sindbad stopped, and gave Hindbad a purse of money, bidding him return the next day, and hear the story of the next voyage. This was repeated each day, till all the voyages were described.

17. **What did Sindbad resolve to do after his father's death?**
    A. spend his inheritance
    B. travel the world
    C. walk in his father's ways
    D. start a new business

18. **Where did Sindbad and the other merchants disembark from their ship for the first time after setting sail?**
    A. the capital of the island
    B. an island in the Indies
    C. the back of a sea monster
    D. Bussorah port

19. **What happened while Sindbad and the merchants were eating and resting on the small island?**
    A. pirates attacked their ship
    B. a sea monster appeared
    C. the island trembled and shook
    D. a storm approached

20. **Who were the people Sindbad met in the cave on the island?**
    A. grooms belonging to the sovereign
    B. natives of the neighboring island
    C. pirates inhabiting the island
    D. other survivors from the sunken ship

21. What is the meaning of the phrase "a good name is better than precious ointment"?
    A. A good reputation is better than expensive ointment which wears off with time
    B. A good name is not as expensive as an ointment
    C. A good name is more difficult to achieve than outer beauty
    D. A good name fades away with time, but it is beautiful while it lasts

22. Which of the following sentences best represents the meaning of "inclined" as used in Para 2?
    A. She listened to her favourite song with her eyes closed and her head inclined, resting on the window.
    B. The Great Pyramid inclines at an angle of about 51.5 degrees to the top
    C. We hiked up a steep incline to the waterfall
    D. His love of books inclined him toward a literary career.

23. What is the meaning of a sloop?
    A. a fore-and-aft rigged boat with one mast and a single jib
    B. the diameter of the stop in an optical system that determines the diameter of the bundle of rays traversing the instrument
    C. a hole or excavation in the ground made by an animal (such as a rabbit) for shelter and habitation
    D. to hide in or as if in a hole in the ground made by an animal for shelter and habitation

24. What is the main idea of paragraph 10?
    A. The captain could not recognize Sindbad because of his clothes
    B. The captain refused to return Sindbad's possessions
    C. The captain believed that Sinbad was dead, and therefore he thought that the man was an imposter
    D. The captain refused to trust him and told him to go back

25. Which of the following items did he not bring back with him?
    A. Wood of aloes
    B. Ginger ale
    C. Pepper
    D. Camphor

THE ADVENTURES OF TOM SAWYER

By Mark Twain

"Tom!"

No answer.

"TOM!"

No answer.

"What's gone with that boy, I wonder? You TOM!"

No answer.

The old lady pulled her spectacles down and looked over them about the room; then she put them up and looked out under them. She seldom or never looked *through* them for so small a thing as a boy; they were her state pair, the pride of her heart, and were built for "style," not service—she could have seen through a pair of stove-lids just as well. She looked perplexed for a moment, and then said, not fiercely, but still loud enough for the furniture to hear:

"Well, I lay if I get hold of you I'll—"

She did not finish, for by this time she was bending down and punching under the bed with the broom, and so she needed breath to punctuate the punches with. She resurrected nothing but the cat.

"I never did see the beat of that boy!"

She went to the open door and stood in it and looked out among the tomato vines and "jimpson" weeds that constituted the garden. No Tom. So she lifted up her voice at an angle calculated for distance and shouted:

"Y-o-u-u TOM!"

There was a slight noise behind her and she turned just in time to seize a small boy by the slack of his roundabout and arrest his flight.

"There! I might 'a' thought of that closet. What you been doing in there?"

"Nothing."

"Nothing! Look at your hands. And look at your mouth. What *is* that truck?"

"I don't know, aunt."

"Well, I know. It's jam—that's what it is. Forty times I've said if you didn't let that jam alone I'd skin you. Hand me that switch."

The switch hovered in the air—the peril was desperate—

"My! Look behind you, aunt!"

The old lady whirled round, and snatched her skirts out of danger. The lad fled on the instant, scrambled up the high board-fence, and disappeared over it.

His aunt Polly stood surprised a moment, and then broke into a gentle laugh.

"Hang the boy, can't I never learn anything? Ain't he played me tricks enough like that for me to be looking out for him by this time? But old fools is the biggest fools there is. Can't learn an old dog new tricks, as the saying is. But my goodness, he never plays them alike, two days, and how is a body to know what's coming? He 'pears to know just how long he can torment me before I get my dander up, and he knows if he can make out to put me off for a minute or make me laugh, it's all down again and I can't hit him a lick. I ain't doing my duty by that boy, and that's the Lord's truth, goodness knows. Spare the rod and spile the child, as the Good Book says. I'm a laying up sin and suffering for us both, I know. He's full of the Old Scratch, but laws-a-me! he's my own dead sister's boy, poor thing, and I ain't got the heart to lash him, somehow. Every time I let him off, my conscience does hurt me so, and every time I hit him my old heart most breaks. Well-a-well, man that is born of woman is of few days and full of trouble, as the Scripture says, and I reckon it's so. He'll play hookey this evening, I'll just be obliged to make him work, tomorrow, to punish him. It's mighty hard to make him work Saturdays, when all the boys are having holiday, but he hates work more than he hates anything else, and I've *got* to do some of my duty by him, or I'll be the ruination of the child."

26. Why did the old lady put her spectacles on?
  A. To look around the room
  B. To read a book
  C. To see through stove lids
  D. To find Tom

27. Where does the old lady go to look for Tom?
  A. The garden
  B. The closet
  C. The kitchen
  D. Under the cabinet

28. 'Ain't he played me tricks enough like that for me to be looking out for him by this time?' What does 'that' refer to in this sentence?
  A. Teasing the cat
  B. Hiding in the closet
  C. Tricking her and then distracting her
  D. Running away from her

29. What does Aunt Polly mean by 'spare the rod and spile the child'?
  A. If you spare a child from discipline, they will be strong
  B. If you spare a child from punishment, they will be grateful
  C. If you use a rod to discipline a child, they will become rebellious
  D. If you don't discipline a child, they will become spoiled

30. What reason does Aunt Polly give for making Tom work on Saturdays?
  A. To teach him the value of hard work
  B. To help with household chores
  C. To keep him busy
  D. To do her duty by him as his guardian

31. How does Aunt Polly feel every time she lets Tom off without punishment?
    A. She feels proud
    B. Her conscience hurts
    C. She feels relief
    D. She feels happy

32. 'He' pears to know just how long he can torment me before I get my dander up, and he knows if he can make out to put me off for a minute or make me laugh, it's all down again and I can't hit him a lick.' What does 'make out' mean in this context?
    A. Make disappear
    B. Succeed in
    C. Make up
    D. Make fun of

33. According to Aunt Polly, a man who is 'born of woman' is:
    A. Strong and resilient
    B. Always happy
    C. Bound for success
    D. Of few days and full of trouble

34. What does Aunt Polly fear she will do if she doesn't discipline Tom?
    A. Be the ruination of the child
    B. Lose control
    C. Anger other family members
    D. Make him unhappy

JANE GOODALL

1. Jane Goodall was a legendary scientist, conservationist and humanitarian who worked tirelessly and made many groundbreaking discoveries that have shaped our understanding of what it means to be human. From 1960 to 1995, without any formal academic training she spent remarkable years devoted to studying chimpanzees in the forests of Gombe Stream National Park in Tanzania and became one of the world's most respected and influential zoologists. She began her research alone in the middle of the tropical forest in Tanzania, East Africa, and steadily built up one of the foremost centers for field research on primates.

2. The British ethologist and conservationist had always dreamt of studying wildlife in Africa and that ambition never failed. In 1957, she embarked on a trip to Kenya with her savings and approached the famous anthropologist Louis Leakey and told him about her wish to work in Africa. She was then appointed as his secretary. Leakey helped her by raising funds for her to become begin a research project program at Gombe, Tanzania.

3. At a time when the world knew very little about chimpanzees and much less about the unique genetic kinship that the species share with humans, she took a very unorthodox approach when most primatologists studied captive animals in zoos. Instead, she immersed herself in their habitat and their lives, to experience life as a neighbor rather than a distant observer. Thus, coming to understand them not only as a species but also as individuals with emotions and long-term bonds.

4. She was fascinated by the way themes used sounds gestures and expressions to communicate with each other. Every noise conveyed a different message and gestures in body movements were also forms of communication. She observed how body movements act as visual display of emotion and intent. For example, males issue threats to rivals by charging forward with their fur raised, often dragging branches of throwing stones or groups of chimps reacting to the coming of rainfall with an "agitated rain dance". She observed that the chips would often pat, embrace or kiss as a way of coming distressed individuals; they would also groom each other's fur which has a coming effect and strengthen social bonds.

5. She spent days in the forest alone with the chimpanzees. Gradually she won their confidence and they accepted her. She filled her notebooks with descriptions of chimpanzees and wrote freely of the emotions, personalities and intelligence of the chimps. One of her most startling discoveries was that wild chimps were good toolmakers. They could use objects as tools, often modifying them to suit their purpose. She saw them stripping twigs to make probes for fishing termites from their nests and chewing clumps of leaves to make sponges for getting water from shallow pools.

6. She championed the cause of chimpanzee conservation and campaigned for better conditions for captive chimps. In 1977, she launched the Jane Goodall Institution for Wildlife Research Education and Conservation in the USA which also has branches in the UK, Canada and Tanzania. Although she stopped doing fieldwork in 1986, she still works hard as a conservationist today, travelling approximately 300 days a year, to raise awareness and money to protect the chimpanzees and their habitats through her non-profit organization.

35. How did Jane Goodall approach her research on chimpanzees?
   A. By conducting experiments in a lab
   B. By observing captive chimps in zoos
   C. By reading previous studies on chimpanzees
   D. By immersing herself in their habitat

36. What did Jane Goodall observe regarding the communication methods of chimpanzees?
   A. Chimpanzees rely solely on smells to communicate
   B. Body movements act as visual displays of emotion and intent
   C. Chimpanzees communicate using a unique form of sign language
   D. Chimpanzees use complex vocalizations to communicate

37. How did wild chimps use tools, according to Jane Goodall's observations?
   A. They stripped twigs and made probes and chewed leaves to make sponges
   B. They used rocks as weapons for hunting
   C. They used flinty to make fire and sharpen other tools
   D. They built structures for shelter using branches

38. What is Jane Goodall's current role?
   A. Anthropologist
   B. Conservationist
   C. Zoologist
   D. Primatologist

39. Which of the following best describes Jane Goodall's approach to studying chimpanzees?
   A. She observed them from a distance without any interaction
   B. She studied them only as a species not as individuals
   C. She came to understand them as individuals with emotions and long-term bonds
   D. She focused solely on their genetic kinship with humans

40. What did Jane Goodall do alone in the forest with the chimpanzees?
   A. Spent days observing and interacting with them
   B. Collected DNA samples for genetic analysis
   C. Brought them back to her camp for further study
   D. Documented their behavior from a distance using cameras

41. What was one of Jane Goodall's most surprising discoveries about wild chimps?
   A. They had a highly developed spoken language
   B. They could communicate using complex vocalizations
   C. They were capable of simple mathematical calculations
   D. They were good toolmakers

42. **What can be a suitable subheading for Para 6?**
    A. Jane's notebook
    B. Who is Jane Goodall?
    C. Observations that Jane made about chimps
    D. Her present contributions

THE WHITE TIGER

1. A special kind of coloring in Asian mainland tigers is called leucistic pigmentation, which makes them look white or bleached, like a white tiger. In the Indian states of Madhya Pradesh, Assam, West Bengal, Bihar, and Odisha, as well as in the Sunderbans region and particularly in the old State of Rewa, it is occasionally known to exist in the wild. Although it bears the classic black tiger stripes, the rest of its coat is white or nearly white.

2. The colour of the white Bengal tigers' fur makes them stand out from other tigers. The absence of the pigment pheomelanin, which is present in Bengal tigers with orange-colored fur, results in white fur. The white Bengal tigers have a **propensity** to grow more quickly and heavily than the orange Bengal tigers. They also have a tendency to be a little bit bigger as adults and at delivery. When they are between two and three years old, white Bengal tigers are completely matured. The white Bengal tiger's stripes, like those of other tigers, are unique and differ from one individual to the next. The tiger's stripes are a skin pigment, thus even after shaving, the animal would retain its distinguishing coat pattern.

3. Both parents must possess the uncommon gene for white coloring, which only naturally occurs roughly once per 10,000 births, for a white Bengal tiger to be born. In addition to having been historically observed in several other subspecies, dark-striped white individuals are well-documented in the Bengal tiger subspecies (*Panthera tigris*). Several hundred white tigers are kept in captivity at this time, with roughly 100 of them located in India. They are well-liked in zoos and entertainment that features exotic animals due to their distinctive white colour fur. Because white tigers don't have adequate camouflage, they are less able to follow prey or evade other predators, which may further contribute to their rarity. The recessive allele in white tigers is the product of a single mutation. (Downes 2021)

4. A second genetic disorder may cause a tiger to have nearly no stripes at all, turning it almost completely white. Georges Cuvier wrote about one such specimen that was on display at Exeter Change in England in 1820, stating that "A white variety of Tiger is sometimes seen, with the stripes very opaque, and not to be observed except in certain angles of light." ."A completely white tiger, with the stripe pattern only being visible under reflected light, similar to the pattern of a white tabby cat, was displayed in the Exeter Change Menagerie in 1820, according to Hamilton Smith. John George Wood described the animal as "creamy white," with the typical tigrine stripes being so faintly marked that they were only visible in certain lights.

5. The numerous brother-sister unions between Bhim and Sumita at the Cincinnati Zoo produced the contemporary strain of snow-white tigers. Their partially Siberian ancestor Tony may have possessed the gene in question. The stripe less phenotype is thought to be the result of a recessive gene becoming homozygous due to continued inbreeding, thus increasing the probability of a white cub. The number of stripe less children born to Bhim and Sumita was about one-fourth. They may possibly have produced children with the gene for the stripe less phenotype, which have been sold to zoos all over the world and are striped white. The gene may also be present in other captive white tigers because Tony's genome can be found in numerous white tiger pedigrees. Due to this, striped-free white tigers have been spotted in zoos as far-flung as the Czech Republic (Liberec), Spain, and Mexico. Stage magicians like Siegfried & Roy have even utilized them.

43. What is the cause of white fur in white Bengal tigers?
    A. Genetic mutation in other pigmentation genes
    B. Exposure to sunlight for long durations
    C. Absence of the pigment pheomelanin
    D. Excessive presence of pheomelanin

44. How do white Bengal tigers compare to orange Bengal tigers in terms of growth?
    A. White Bengal tigers grow more quickly and heavily
    B. Orange Bengal tigers grow more rapidly
    C. White and Orange Bengal tigers have similar growth rates
    D. White Bengal tigers and Orange Bengal tigers grow at the same pace initially, but after a certain age, the growth of White Bengal tigers slows down.

45. What makes white Bengal tigers less capable of following prey or evading predators?
    A. Lack of strength and agility
    B. Poor eyesight
    C. Soft and noisy footsteps
    D. Inadequate camouflage due to their white colour fur

46. How rare is the occurrence of white Bengal tigers in the wild?
    A. Approximately once per 100 births
    B. Once in a million births
    C. Almost every other birth
    D. Approximately once per 10,000 births

47. What is one possible consequence of prolonged inbreeding in white tigers?
    A. Change in eye coloration patterns
    B. Higher occurrence of genetic disorders
    C. Decreased fertility among the tigers
    D. Increased probability of offspring with stripe less phenotype

48. Which of the following words is a synonym of 'propensity'?
    A. Proneness
    B. Premonition
    C. Propagation
    D. Prejudice

49. How did Georges Cuvier describe the stripes of the white tiger he observed?
    A. Opaque and visible only in certain angles of light
    B. Clear and easily distinguishable
    C. Colourless and translucent
    D. Refractive and shimmering in all lights

50. Which of the Paras talks about another anomaly in white tigers that renders them stripe less?
    A. Para 2 & 4
    B. Para 1 & 3
    C. Para 3 & 4
    D. Para 4 & 5

Grade 5
ELA Practice Test 4

A Morning Adventure

1. Although the morning was raw, and although the fog still seemed heavy—I say seemed, for the windows were so encrusted with dirt that they would have made midsummer sunshine dim—I was sufficiently forewarned of the discomfort within doors at that early hour and sufficiently curious about London to think it a good idea on the part of Miss Jellyby when she proposed that we should go out for a walk.

2. "Ma won't be down for ever so long," she said, "and then it's a chance if breakfast's ready for an hour afterwards, they dawdle so. As to Pa, he gets what he can and goes to the office. He never has what you would call a regular breakfast. Priscilla leaves him out the loaf and some milk, when there is any, overnight. Sometimes there isn't any milk, and sometimes the cat drinks it. But I'm afraid you must be tired, Miss Summerson, and perhaps you would rather go to bed."

3. "I am not at all tired, my dear," said I, "and would much prefer to go out."

4. "If you're sure you would," returned Miss Jellyby, "I'll get my things on."

5. Ada said she would go too, and was soon astir. I made a proposal to Peepy, in default of being able to do anything better for him, that he should let me wash him and afterwards lay him down on my bed again. To this he submitted with the best grace possible, staring at me during the whole operation as if he never had been, and never could again be, so astonished in his life—looking very miserable also, certainly, but making no complaint, and going snugly to sleep as soon as it was over. At first I was in two minds about taking such a liberty, but I soon reflected that nobody in the house was likely to notice it.

6. What with the bustle of dispatching Peepy and the bustle of getting myself ready and helping Ada, I was soon quite in a glow. We found Miss Jellyby trying to warm herself at the fire in the writing-room, which Priscilla was then lighting with a smutty parlour candlestick, throwing the candle in to make it burn better. Everything was just as we had left it last night and was evidently intended to remain so. Below-stairs the dinner-cloth had not been taken away, but had been left ready for breakfast. Crumbs, dust, and waste-paper were all over the house. Some pewter pots and a milk-can hung on the area railings; the door stood open; and we met the cook round the corner coming out of a public-house, wiping her mouth. She mentioned, as she passed us, that she had been to see what o'clock it was.

(ADAPTED FROM: BLEAK HOUSE, CHARLES DICKENS)

1. What is the reason the windows appeared dim despite the sunshine outside?

A. The morning was extremely cold
B. The windows were encrusted with dirt
C. There was heavy fog outside
D. The windows were tinted

2. What does Miss Jellyby suggest they do at that early hour in the morning?

　A. Go out for a walk
　B. Have breakfast
　C. Clean the windows
　D. Take a nap

3. How does Miss Jellyby describe her father's breakfast routine?

　A. He has a regular breakfast every morning
　B. He eats whatever is available at the time
　C. He skips breakfast and goes straight to the office
　D. He prefers milk and bread for breakfast

4. What condition was the house in when they came downstairs?

　A. Clean and tidy
　B. Cluttered with toys
　C. Dusty and messy
　D. Freshly painted

5. Where did the cook go before meeting the others?

　A. The grocery store
　B. The public-house
　C. The bakery
　D. The park

6. Which word from paragraph 2 means 'to waste time'?

　A. Loaf
　B. Dawdle
　C. Grounded
　D. None of the above

7. What prompts Miss Jellyby and the narrator to go for a walk in the morning?

　A. The desire for a breath of fresh air
　B. The anticipation of a well-prepared breakfast
　C. The uncomfortable conditions indoors
　D. The need to visit a local market

8. Why does the narrator decide to wash Peepy?

A. Because Peepy was covered in dirt and needed cleaning
B. Because Peepy requested to be washed
C. Because it was a customary morning routine
D. Because the house was too dirty for Peepy to stay indoors

A Useful Minister

1. About half-past ten the cracked bell of the small church began to ring, and presently the people began to gather for the morning sermon. The Sunday-school children distributed themselves about the house and occupied pews with their parents, so as to be under supervision. Aunt Polly came, and Tom and Sid and Mary sat with her—Tom being placed next the aisle, in order that he might be as far away from the open window and the seductive outside summer scenes as possible.

2. The crowd filed up the aisles: the aged and needy postmaster, who had seen better days; the mayor and his wife—for they had a mayor there, among other unnecessaries; the justice of the peace; the widow Douglas, fair, smart, and forty, a generous, good-hearted soul and well-to-do, her hill mansion the only palace in the town, and the most hospitable and much the most lavish in the matter of festivities that St. Petersburg could boast; the bent and venerable Major and Mrs. Ward; lawyer Riverson, the new notable from a distance; next the belle of the village, followed by a troop of lawn-clad and ribbon-decked young heart-breakers; then all the young clerks in town in a body—for they had stood in the vestibule sucking their cane-heads, a circling wall of oiled and simpering admirers, till the last girl had run their gantlet; and last of all came the Model Boy, Willie Mufferson, taking as heedful care of his mother as if she were cut glass. He always brought his mother to church, and was the pride of all the matrons. The boys all hated him, he was so good. And besides, he had been "thrown up to them" so much. His white handkerchief was hanging out of his pocket behind, as usual on Sundays   accidentally. Tom had no handkerchief, and he looked upon boys who had as snobs.

3. The congregation being fully assembled, now, the bell rang once more, to warn laggards and stragglers, and then a solemn hush fell upon the church which was only broken by the tittering and whispering of the choir in the gallery. The choir always tittered and whispered all through service. There was once a church choir that was not ill-bred, but I have forgotten where it was, now. It was a great many years ago, and I can scarcely remember anything about it, but I think it was in some foreign country.

4. The minister gave out the hymn, and read it through with a relish, in a peculiar style which was much admired in that part of the country. His voice began on a medium key and climbed steadily up till it reached a certain point, where it bore with strong emphasis upon the topmost word and then plunged down as if from a spring-board.

(ADAPTED FROM: THE ADVENTURES OF TOM SAWYER, MARK TWAIN)

9. Why was Tom placed next to the aisle during the sermon?

A. He liked the view outside the window
B. He needed to be supervised by the Sunday-school children
C. He wanted to sit close to his family
D. He wanted to be far away from the outside scenes

10. Who is described as the "belle of the village" in the passage?

A. Aunt Polly
B. The widow Douglas
C. Mary
D. Willie Mufferson

11. Why did the boys in town hate Willie Mufferson?

A. He was rich and spoiled
B. He was always tittering and whispering during service
C. He was good and was praised by everyone
D. He didn't have a handkerchief on Sundays

12. How did the minister read the hymn in a peculiar style?

A. He sang it in a foreign language
B. He read it with strong emphasis on certain words
C. He read it slowly and monotonously
D. He read it in a medium key throughout

13. Who among the congregation is described as generous, good-hearted, and well-to-do?

A. The mayor
B. Lawyer Riverson
C. The widow Douglas
D. The aged and needy postmaster

14. Why did the boys think having a handkerchief on Sundays made one a snob?

A. They believed it was a sign of wealth and vanity
B. They considered it a gesture of showing off
C. They associated it with foreign customs
D. They thought it was unnecessary and pretentious

15. Dictionary meanings of the word: _hospitable_ (PARA 2)

1. a person who is friendly and welcoming

2. a suitable place

   A. 1
   B. 2
   C. Both 1 &2
   D. Neither 1 nor 2

16. In paragraph 3, what does the word "tittering" mean?

   A. A deep and serious sound
   B. A musical tone
   C. A suppressed laugh
   D. A loud chatter

NORTHAMPTON

1. The little girl performed her long journey in safety; and at Northampton was met by Mrs. Norris, who thus regaled in the credit of being foremost to welcome her, and in the importance of leading her into the others, and recommending her to their kindness.

2. Fanny Price was at this time just ten years old, and though there might not be much in her first appearance to captivate, there was, at least, nothing to disgust her relations. She was small of her age, with no glow of complexion, nor any other striking beauty; exceedingly timid and shy, and shrinking from notice; but her air, though awkward, was not vulgar, her voice was sweet, and when she spoke her countenance was pretty. Sir Thomas and Lady Bertram received her very kindly; and Sir Thomas, seeing how much she needed encouragement, tried to be all that was conciliating: but he had to work against a most untoward gravity of deportment; and Lady Bertram, without taking half so much trouble, or speaking one word where he spoke ten, by the mere aid of a good-humored smile, became immediately the less awful character of the two.

3. The young people were all at home, and sustained their share in the introduction very well, with much good humour, and no embarrassment, at least on the part of the sons, who, at seventeen and sixteen, and tall of their age, had all the grandeur of men in the eyes of their little cousin. The two girls were more at a loss from being younger and in greater awe of their father, who addressed them on the occasion with rather an injudicious particularity. But they were too much used to company and praise to have anything like natural shyness; and their confidence increasing from their cousin's total want of it, they were soon able to take a full survey of her face and her frock in easy indifference.

4. They were a remarkably fine family, the sons very well-looking, the daughters decidedly handsome, and all of them well-grown and forward of their age, which produced as striking a difference between the cousins in person, as education had given to their address; and no one would have supposed the girls so nearly of an age as they really were. There were in fact but two years between the youngest and Fanny. Julia Bertram was only twelve, and Maria but a year older.

5. The little visitor meanwhile was as unhappy as possible. Afraid of everybody, ashamed of herself, and longing for the home she had left, she knew not how to look up, and could scarcely speak to be heard, or without crying. Mrs. Norris had been talking to her the whole way from Northampton of her wonderful good fortune, and the extraordinary degree of gratitude and good behavior which it ought to produce, and her consciousness of misery was therefore increased by the idea of its being a wicked thing for her not to be happy. The fatigue, too, of so long a journey, became soon no trifling evil.

6. In vain were the well-meant of Sir Thomas, and all the declarations of Mrs. Norris that she would be a good girl; in vain did Lady Bertram smile and make her sit on the sofa with herself and pug, and vain was even the sight of a gooseberry tart towards giving her comfort; she could scarcely swallow two mouthfuls before tears interrupted her, and sleep seeming to be her likeliest friend, she was taken to finish her sorrows in bed.

(ADAPTED FROM: MANSFIELD PARK, JANE AUSTEN)

17. How did Mrs. Norris feel about being the first to welcome the little girl?

  A. Annoyed
  B. Proud and important
  C. Jealous
  D. Indifferent

18. How did Sir Thomas try to interact with Fanny Price?

  A. He ignored her completely.
  B. He was unkind and stern.
  C. He tried to be kind and conciliating.
  D. He scolded her for being timid.

19. How did the sons of the family treat their little cousin?

  A. With awe and shyness
  B. With good humor and no embarrassment
  C. With indifference and rudeness
  D. With jealousy and envy

20. Why were the two girls more at a loss compared to the boys in the introduction?

  A. They were younger and more fearful of their father.
  B. They were not used to company and praise.
  C. They were not well-grown and forward of their age.
  D. They were not as good-looking as their cousins.

21. What was the age gap between Fanny and the youngest cousin?

   A. 1 year
   B. 2 years
   C. 10 years
   D. 12 years

22. Why was the little girl unhappy despite being told of her "wonderful good fortune" and the need to be happy?

   A. She missed her home and felt ashamed of herself.
   B. She was not properly welcomed by her cousins.
   C. She was tired from the journey and needed rest.
   D. She was upset about being away from Mrs. Norris.

23. How do the daughters' ages and appearances compare to their cousin Fanny's?

   A. The daughters are older and less attractive than Fanny.
   B. The daughters are younger and more attractive than Fanny.
   C. The daughters are the same age and equally attractive as Fanny.
   D. The daughters are slightly older and equally attractive as Fanny.

24. Which paragraph describes Fanny Price's physical appearance and demeanor when she first arrived at Northampton?

   A. Paragraph 1
   B. Paragraph 2
   C. Paragraph 3
   D. Paragraph 4

25. Identify the affixes in: *encouragement*

   A. suffix: ent
   B. prefix: encourage
   C. prefix: en, suffix: ment
   D. prefix: encourage, suffix: ent

The Coral Reef Ecosystem

Coral reefs, nature's underwater masterpieces, flourish in the warm and shallow waters of oceans across the globe. Renowned as the "rainforests of the sea," these ecosystems captivate with their remarkable diversity and exquisite beauty. An exploration of the coral reef ecosystem unveils the intricacies of its components and the significance it holds in our planet's aquatic realm.

Coral Polyps: At the heart of coral reefs are coral polyps, minuscule organisms that play a pivotal role in reef construction. These extraordinary creatures secrete calcium carbonate, a process that results in the formation of the coral's robust skeleton. As these skeletons accumulate over time, they collectively craft the structural framework of the entire reef. Each coral polyp is a living entity, contributing its distinct touch to the exquisite mosaic of the coral ecosystem.

Marine Life: The coral reefs teem with a rich diversity of marine life, creating an underwater haven for an array of species. Among the vibrant inhabitants are various species of fish, each adapted to the intricacies of the reef's ecosystem. Sea turtles, graceful and ancient wanderers of the oceans, seek refuge among the coral crevices. Crustaceans and mollusks, intricate and fascinating in their forms, find homes within the coral's intricate architecture. The corals' crevices and niches provide shelter and sanctuaries for these creatures, fostering a complex web of interactions.

Algae and Coral Symbiosis: Beneath the surface of this underwater realm, an intricate partnership thrives. Corals and algae, specifically the zooxanthellae, engage in a symbiotic relationship that is vital for the coral's survival. These microscopic algae take residence within the coral tissues, harnessing sunlight to perform photosynthesis. Through this process, they provide the corals with essential energy and nutrients. In return, the corals offer the algae a secure home and a steady supply of necessary substances.

Biodiversity Hotspots: Despite covering only a fraction of the ocean floor, coral reefs stand as biodiversity hotspots. Astonishingly, they host about a quarter of all marine species on the planet. This incredible diversity spans from the tiniest invertebrates to the majestic marine mammals. The intricate labyrinth of coral formations, with their myriad hiding spots and sources of nourishment, supports an unparalleled array of life forms.

Threats to Coral Reefs: Regrettably, coral reefs face grave challenges due to human activities. Climate change, driven by rising temperatures and ocean acidification, poses a significant threat. Overfishing disrupts the delicate balance of the ecosystem, while pollution, originating both from land and sea, further deteriorates reef health. Tourist activities and coastal developments inflict physical damage, exacerbating the perilous situation. These factors culminate in coral bleaching events, causing a decline in the vibrancy and vitality of coral ecosystems.

Conservation Efforts: Recognizing the critical importance of coral reefs, dedicated efforts are being made to safeguard and preserve them. Organizations and governments are collaborating to establish marine protected areas, where stringent regulations limit human impact. Strategies to regulate fishing practices and reduce pollution aim to restore and sustain the delicate equilibrium of the reef ecosystem. Public awareness campaigns emphasize the significance of these underwater marvels, fostering a sense of responsibility for their well-being.

The coral reef ecosystem, a testament to nature's ingenuity, beckons us to delve deeper into its intricate workings and vital role in the marine realm. Amidst the challenges it faces, united efforts can ensure that these vibrant ecosystems continue to thrive, offering a haven of life, beauty, and wonder beneath the waves.

26. What are coral polyps primarily responsible for in the coral reef ecosystem?
   A. Providing energy through photosynthesis.
   B. Forming the hard coral skeleton.
   C. Regulating the temperature of ocean water.
   D. Acting as a shelter for marine animals.

27. Why are coral reefs often referred to as "rainforests of the sea"?
   A. Because they experience frequent rainfall.
   B. Because they are found near rainforests on land.
   C. Because they exhibit similar levels of biodiversity as rainforests.
   D. Because they are covered in vegetation like rainforests.

28. Which of the following accurately describes the mutualistic relationship between corals and algae (zooxanthellae) mentioned in the passage?
   A. Corals provide energy to algae through photosynthesis.
   B. Algae provide corals with shelter and nutrients.
   C. Corals and algae compete for resources in the reef ecosystem.
   D. Algae consume corals' excess nutrients.

29. What role does the coral skeleton play in the formation of a coral reef?
   A. It provides a hiding place for marine life.
   B. It serves as a food source for algae.
   C. It contributes to the structure and framework of the reef.
   D. It absorbs excess sunlight to protect the coral polyps.

30. Why are coral reefs considered biodiversity hotspots, despite covering a relatively small area of the ocean floor?
   A. Coral reefs harbor the majority of marine species.
   B. Coral reefs are the primary breeding grounds for marine life.
   C. Coral reefs have a unique ability to regenerate damaged ecosystems.
   D. Coral reefs provide a habitat for terrestrial as well as aquatic species.

31. Which of the following is identified as a significant threat to coral reefs in the passage?
    A. Volcanic activity leading to habitat destruction.
    B. Acid rain causing erosion of coral skeletons.
    C. Overconsumption of algae by marine life.
    D. Pollution resulting from coastal development and tourism.

32. How do conservation efforts aim to protect and preserve coral reefs?
    A. By relocating coral reefs to controlled environments.
    B. By promoting fishing practices that exploit coral reefs sustainably.
    C. By creating awareness about the beauty of coral reefs.
    D. By establishing marine protected areas and regulating human activities.

33. What is the primary cause of coral bleaching and decline in reef health, as mentioned in the passage?
    A. Marine protected areas
    B. Algae and coral symbiosis
    C. Climate change and human activities
    D. Biodiversity hotspots

The Inspiring Journey of Mahatma Gandhi

1. Mohandas Karamchand Gandhi, better known as Mahatma Gandhi, was one of the most influential figures in the history of India and the world. Born on October 2, 1869, in Porbandar, a coastal town in present-day Gujarat, India, Gandhi's life was marked by a relentless pursuit of truth, non-violence, and the struggle for India's independence from British rule.

2. From an early age, Gandhi exhibited a strong sense of justice and compassion. He was a disciplined student who valued honesty and simplicity. After completing his education in law in London, he returned to India and began practicing law in South Africa, where he witnessed racial discrimination against Indians. This experience sparked his interest in fighting for civil rights and social justice.

3. It was in South Africa that Gandhi first employed his philosophy of non-violent resistance, which he called "Satyagraha" or "truth-force." Through peaceful protests, strikes, and civil disobedience, he successfully fought against unjust laws and gained the respect and admiration of people worldwide.

4. In 1915, Gandhi returned to India and soon became a prominent leader in the Indian National Congress. He advocated for the rights of farmers, workers, and oppressed communities, using non-violent methods to challenge British colonial rule. He encouraged Indians to boycott British goods and institutions, promoting self-reliance and the use of local resources.

5. One of Gandhi's most significant contributions to India's struggle for independence was the Salt March in 1930. In response to the oppressive British salt tax, he led a 240-mile-long march to the Arabian Sea, symbolically making salt from seawater. This act of civil disobedience inspired millions of Indians to join the freedom movement.

6. Throughout his life, Gandhi emphasized the value of self-discipline and self-sufficiency. He promoted the use of traditional Indian spinning wheels, or "charkhas," to produce handmade cloth, urging people to boycott British textiles. This movement, known as the "Swadeshi Movement," aimed to strengthen India's economy and foster a sense of national pride.

7. Despite facing numerous arrests and imprisonments, Gandhi remained committed to non-violence. He believed that through love, compassion, and understanding, even the most oppressive regimes could be transformed. His principles of non-violence, truth, and selflessness, collectively known as "Satyagraha," became a powerful force for social change and inspired other civil rights leaders, including Martin Luther King Jr. and Nelson Mandela.

8. Gandhi's efforts culminated in India's independence on August 15, 1947. However, he was deeply saddened by the partition of India, which led to communal violence and the creation of Pakistan. In an attempt to stop the bloodshed, he undertook a fast until all parties agreed to peace and communal harmony.

9. On January 30, 1948, Mahatma Gandhi's life came to a tragic end when he was assassinated by a fanatic. The nation mourned the loss of its beloved leader, but his teachings and principles continued to resonate worldwide.

10. Mahatma Gandhi's legacy extends far beyond India's independence struggle. His ideas of non-violence, social justice, and communal harmony have left an indelible mark on the global stage. He believed that the path to truth and freedom was through love, tolerance, and understanding, which he called "ahimsa" or non-violence. His vision of a world free from hatred and oppression continues to inspire millions around the world, emphasizing the importance of unity, humility, and respect for all beings.

34. What was the main purpose of the Salt March led by Mahatma Gandhi in 1930?

A. To protest against British colonial rule
B. To demand better working conditions for farmers
C. To promote the use of charkhas (spinning wheels)
D. To challenge the salt tax imposed by the British

35. What was the "Swadeshi Movement" promoted by Gandhi during India's struggle for independence?

A. A movement to promote communal harmony
B. A movement to boycott British goods and promote Indian products
C. A movement to demand equal rights for all citizens
D. A movement to improve education and healthcare facilities

36. Choose the synonym for "relentless" from the options below:

A. Cruel
B. Compassionate
C. Persistent
D. Forgiving

37. What is the opposite of Gandhi's philosophy of "ahimsa" or non-violence?

A. Compassion
B. Tolerance
C. Aggression
D. Understanding

38. Based on the passage, why did Gandhi encourage Indians to boycott British goods and institutions?

A. To promote the use of traditional Indian textiles.
B. To strengthen the British economy.
C. To increase reliance on foreign products.
D. To demonstrate loyalty to British colonial rule.

39. Which term can be used interchangeably with "Satyagraha," Gandhi's philosophy of non-violent resistance?

A. Harmony
B. Justice
C. Disobedience
D. War

40. Which event serves as an example of Gandhi's commitment to stopping violence and promoting communal harmony?

A. His participation in the Salt March.
B. His efforts to challenge British colonial rule.
C. His advocacy for civil rights in South Africa.
D. His decision to fast in response to India's partition.

41. *Title of the 2nd Paragraph: "Gandhi's Early Life and Education"*

What does the title "Gandhi's Early Life and Education" suggest is the main focus of the 2nd paragraph?

A. Gandhi's influence on civil rights movements.
B. Gandhi's struggles during his early years.
C. Gandhi's experiences with racial discrimination.
D. Gandhi's achievements as a lawyer in London.

"Wake, Little Brother; I bring news."

1) "Are all well in the jungle?" said Mowgli, hugging him.

2) "All except the wolves that were burned with the Red Flower. Now, listen. Shere Khan has gone away to hunt far off till his coat grows again, for he is badly singed. When he returns, he swears that he will lay thy bones in the Waingunga."

3) "There are two words to that. I also have made a little promise. But news is always good. I am tired to-night, —very tired with new things, Gray Brother, —but bring me the news always."

4) "Thou wilt not forget that thou art a wolf? Men will not make thee forget?" said Gray Brother anxiously.

5) "Never. I will always remember that I love thee and all in our cave. But also I will always remember that I have been cast out of the Pack."

6) "And that thou mayest be cast out of another pack. Men are only men, Little Brother, and their talk is like the talk of frogs in a pond. When I come down here again, I will wait for thee in the bamboos at the edge of the grazing-ground."

7) For three months after that night Mowgli hardly ever left the village gate, he was so busy learning the ways and customs of men. First, he had to wear a cloth round him, which annoyed him horribly; and then he had to learn about money, which he did not in the least understand, and about plowing, of which he did not see the use. Then the little children in the village made him very angry. Luckily, the Law of the Jungle had taught him to keep his temper, for in the jungle life and food depend on keeping your temper; but when they made fun of him because he would not play games or fly kites, or because he mispronounced some word, only the knowledge that it was unsportsmanlike to kill little naked cubs kept him from picking them up and breaking them in two.

8) He did not know his own strength in the least. In the jungle he knew he was weak compared with the beasts, but in the village people said that he was as strong as a bull.

9) And Mowgli had not the faintest idea of the difference that caste makes between man and man. When the potter's donkey slipped in the clay pit, Mowgli hauled it out by the tail, and helped to stack the pots for their journey to the market at Khanhiwara. That was very shocking, too, for the potter is a low-caste man, and his donkey is worse. When the priest scolded him, Mowgli threatened to put him on the donkey too, and the priest told Messua's husband that Mowgli had better be set to work as soon as possible; and the village headman told Mowgli that he would have to go out with the buffaloes next day, and herd them while they grazed. No one was more pleased than Mowgli; and that night because he had been appointed a servant of the village, as it were, he went off to a circle that met every evening on a masonry platform under a great fig-tree. It was the village club, and the headman and the watchman and the barber, who knew all the gossip of the village, and old Buldeo, the village hunter, who had a Tower musket, met and smoked. The monkeys sat and talked in the upper branches, and there was a hole under the platform where a cobra lived, and he had his little platter of milk every night because he was sacred; and the old men sat around the tree and talked and pulled at the big huqas (the water-pipes) till far into the night. They told wonderful tales of gods and men and ghosts; and Buldeo told even more wonderful ones of the ways of beasts in the

jungle, till the eyes of the children sitting outside the circle bulged out of their heads. Most of the tales were about animals, for the jungle was always at their door. The deer and the wild pig grubbed up their crops, and now and again the tiger carried off a man at twilight, within sight of the village gates.

(ADAPTED FROM: THE JUNGLE BOOK, RUDYARD KIPLING)

42. **What has happened to Shere Khan that made him go away?**

    A. He is badly injured in a fight
    B. He is hunting in a distant place
    C. He is angry with Mowgli
    D. He is lost in the jungle

43. **What promise has Mowgli made?**

    A. To become the leader of the wolves
    B. To seek revenge on Shere Khan
    C. To learn the ways of men
    D. To always remember his wolf family

44. **Why does Mowgli resist picking up and breaking the village children?**

    A. He doesn't want to be seen as violent
    B. He fears the consequences of his actions
    C. He knows it's wrong to harm others
    D. He believes the Law of the Jungle forbids it

45. **What does the village head-man ask Mowgli to do?**

    A. Learn about money and plowing
    B. Go to the market at Khanhiwara
    C. Herd the buffaloes while they graze
    D. Join the village club under the fig-tree

46. **What is a common threat to the village according to the passage?**

    A. Wild animals stealing crops
    B. Drought and famine
    C. Ghosts haunting the villagers
    D. Children misbehaving in the jungle

47. **Which word in paragraph 9 means 'indefinite' / 'unclear'?**

    A. Difference
    B. Grazed
    C. Faintest
    D. None of the above

48. Which paragraph describes Mowgli's willingness to learn about human ways and his interaction with the villagers?

    A. Paragraph 3
    B. Paragraph 4
    C. Paragraph 5
    D. Paragraph 6

49. Why did Mowgli feel pleased after being appointed a servant of the village?

    A. He enjoyed herding buffaloes.
    B. He wanted to meet the old men in the village club.
    C. He liked being part of village discussions.
    D. He was excited to work with the potter.

50. What could be a suitable title for the last paragraph of the passage?

    A. "Tales of Gods and Men"
    B. "The Village Gathering"
    C. "Buldeo's Jungle Stories"
    D. "Nighttime Conversations"

Grade 5 Answer Key

Grade 5

Ans keys

The Magical Quern and the Salted Sea

1. **B) To ask for help**

The poor brother went to his rich brother on Christmas Eve to ask for help. The story mentions that the poor brother had nothing to celebrate the festive season, so he approached his rich brother in the hope of receiving assistance. The poor brother was in a difficult situation and needed support from his wealthy sibling. This choice is correct because it directly aligns with the poor brother's intention and the reason for his visit.

The other choices are incorrect because they do not accurately reflect the events and motivations described in the story. Choice A, "To celebrate the festive season together," is incorrect because the poor brother had nothing to celebrate and was seeking help, not a celebration. Choice C, "To exchange gifts," is incorrect because there is no mention of any gift exchange between the brothers in the story. Choice D, "To share a meal," is incorrect because although it is Christmas Eve, the poor brother's primary objective was to ask for help, not to share a meal with his brother.

2. **D) A flitch of bacon**

The rich brother promised to give the poor brother a flitch of bacon in return for a favor. In the story, the poor brother approached his rich brother on Christmas Eve, seeking help. The rich brother, though not pleased to see him, made a deal and promised the poor brother a whole flitch of bacon if he agreed to do something for him. This choice is correct because it accurately represents the promised reward mentioned in the story.

The other choices are incorrect because they do not correspond to what the rich brother promised. Choice A, "A magical quern," is incorrect because the quern was the item that the poor brother had to obtain as part of the favor, not the promised reward. Choice B, "A feast for Christmas," is incorrect because there is no mention of the rich brother offering a feast as a reward. Choice C, "A golden house," is incorrect because the poor brother later uses the magical quern's power to build a golden house, but it was not promised by the rich brother in exchange for the favor.

3. **C) In the Devil's dwelling**

The poor brother found a bright light in the Devil's dwelling on his journey. After walking all day, he eventually entered Hell and stumbled upon a bright light within the Devil's dwelling. It was there that he encountered an old man with a long white beard who offered him advice. This choice is correct because it accurately reflects the location where the poor brother discovered the bright light.

The other choices are incorrect because they do not align with the events described in the story. Choice A, "In a dark cave," is incorrect because the poor brother did not find the bright light in a cave but rather within the Devil's dwelling. Choice B, "In his brother's house," is incorrect because there is no mention of the bright light being found in the rich brother's house. Choice D, "In the forest," is incorrect because the story does not mention the bright light being located in a forest.

Grade 5

Ans keys

4. B) The poor brother encounters an old man in Hell who offers him advice.

The main idea of paragraph 5 is that the poor brother encounters an old man in Hell who offers him advice. The paragraph describes how, after a long journey, the poor brother enters Hell and finds himself surrounded by devils who are eager to buy the flitch of bacon. However, he agrees to sell it only if he receives a magical quern from behind the Devil's door. The paragraph then introduces the old man with a long white beard, who reveals that he is in Hell and offers advice to the poor brother. This choice is correct because it captures the central theme of the paragraph.

The other choices are incorrect because they do not accurately represent the main idea of paragraph 5. Choice A, "The poor brother surprises his wife with the magical quern's abilities," is incorrect because the paragraph does not mention the poor brother returning home or surprising his wife. Choice C, "The poor brother learns how to use the quern on his way back home," is incorrect because the paragraph does not focus on the poor brother's journey back home or his learning process. Choice D, "The poor brother sells the flitch of bacon to devils in Hell," is incorrect because although the poor brother agrees to sell the flitch of bacon, the paragraph does not mention the actual sale taking place in Hell.

5. B) A slab of cured bacon

In the story of the magical quern, the word "flitch" refers to a slab of cured bacon. The story mentions that the poor brother went to his rich brother on Christmas Eve and asked for help. In return, the rich brother made a deal and promised the poor brother a whole flitch of bacon if he agreed to do something for him. This choice is correct because it accurately represents the meaning of "flitch" within the context of the story.

The other choices are incorrect because they do not correspond to the meaning of "flitch" as used in the story. Choice A, "A type of magical object," is incorrect because the story does not describe the flitch as a magical object, but rather as a specific item of food. Choice C, "A piece of furniture," is incorrect because a flitch is not associated with furniture but with food. Choice D, "A hidden door in Hell," is incorrect because the story does not mention a hidden door in Hell being referred to as a flitch.

6. A) With a feast prepared by the quern

The poor brother surprised his wife when he returned home by presenting her with a feast prepared by the magical quern. The story mentions that the poor brother learned how to use the quern on his way back and arrived home late on Christmas Eve. He then surprised his wife with the magical quern's abilities, which allowed them to have an abundance of food. This choice is correct because it accurately represents the way the poor brother surprised his wife upon his return.

The other choices are incorrect because they do not correspond to how the poor brother surprised his wife in the story. Choice B, "With a sack of gold coins," is incorrect because there is no mention of the poor brother bringing a sack of gold coins when he returns home. Choice C, "With a beautiful golden house," is incorrect because the golden house is not mentioned as part of the surprise for his wife but rather as a result of the poor brother's later use of the quern's power. Choice D, "With a magical creature," is incorrect because there is no mention of a magical creature being involved in the surprise.

Grade 5 — Ans keys

7. C) To impress his friends and family

The rich brother wanted to borrow the quern from his poor brother in order to impress his friends and family. In the story, it is mentioned that the rich brother became consumed by envy when he saw the abundance of food and the prosperity that the quern brought to his poor brother's household. He begged his brother to lend him the quern until hay-harvest, promising a hefty sum. This choice is correct because it accurately reflects the rich brother's motivation for wanting to borrow the quern.

The other choices are incorrect because they do not align with the rich brother's intention as described in the story. Choice A, "To build a golden house," is incorrect because the desire to build a golden house is not mentioned as the reason why the rich brother wanted to borrow the quern. Choice B, "To learn its magical abilities," is incorrect because there is no indication that the rich brother wanted to learn how to use the quern. Choice D, "To grind salt for his ship," is incorrect because the purpose of grinding salt for his ship is not mentioned in relation to the rich brother's desire to borrow the quern.

8. C) Paragraph 7

The paragraph that could have the heading "The Envious Brother" is paragraph 7. In this paragraph, the story describes how the rich brother, consumed by envy, begged his poor brother to lend him the magical quern. The rich brother's envy is evident as he witnesses the abundance of food and prosperity brought about by the quern's abilities. He persuades his brother to lend him the quern until hay-harvest, promising a hefty sum. This choice is correct because it captures the central theme of the rich brother's envy and his desire to possess the quern.

The other choices are incorrect because they do not represent the specific content related to the rich brother's envy as described in the story. Choice A, "Paragraph 4," is incorrect because this paragraph describes the poor brother encountering an old man in Hell who offers him advice, which is unrelated to the rich brother's envy. Choice B, "Paragraph 6," is incorrect because this paragraph focuses on the poor brother surprising his wife with the magical quern's abilities, not on the rich brother's envy. Choice D, "Paragraph 9," is incorrect because this paragraph describes the poor brother's wife encountering the overflowing broth, which does not directly relate to the rich brother's envy.

9. D) It continued grinding salt at the bottom of the sea

In the end, the quern continued grinding salt at the bottom of the sea. The story mentions that a skipper came seeking the quern's ability to grind salt, and the poor brother was convinced to sell it. However, the skipper did not learn how to control the quern, resulting in the ship sinking and the quern being lost at the bottom of the sea, where it continues to grind salt to this day. This choice is correct because it accurately represents the fate of the quern as described in the story.

The other choices are incorrect because they do not align with what happened to the quern in the end. Choice A, "It was destroyed by the rich brother," is incorrect because there is no mention of the rich brother destroying the quern. Choice B, "It was returned to the poor brother's house," is incorrect because the story does not state that the quern was returned to the poor brother's house. Choice C, "It was lost during the flood," is incorrect because although there is a flood caused by the quern's uncontrollable grinding, the story does not indicate that the quern itself was lost during the flood.

Grade 5   Ans keys

The Nightingale and The Rose

10. **A) Red roses**

The student's beloved demanded red roses in order to dance with him. In the story, it is mentioned that the student wished to dance with his beloved, and she had promised to dance with him if he brought her red flowers. This choice is correct because it accurately represents the condition set by the student's beloved for their dance.

The other choices are incorrect because they do not align with what the student's beloved demanded in order to dance with him. Choice B, "White flowers," is incorrect because there is no mention of the beloved demanding white flowers. Choice C, "Yellow flowers," is incorrect because there is no mention of the beloved demanding yellow flowers. Choice D, "Precious jewels," is incorrect because although the beloved rejects the red flower given by the student, there is no indication that she demanded precious jewels in order to dance with him.

11. **C) Because she felt sorry for him**

The Nightingale decided to help the student because she felt sorry for him. In the story, it is mentioned that the Nightingale heard the student's sadness and felt sympathy for him. She saw how much he longed for a red flower to bring him joy, and she recognized his genuine passion and love. Filled with kindness and understanding the power of love, the Nightingale was determined to help the student. This choice is correct because it accurately represents the Nightingale's motivation to assist the student.

The other choices are incorrect because they do not align with the Nightingale's actual reason for helping the student. Choice A, "Because she wanted to become his friend," is incorrect because there is no mention of the Nightingale's desire to become the student's friend. Choice B, "Because she wanted him to sing with her," is incorrect because although the Nightingale sang about the student, there is no indication that she helped him with the intention of having him sing with her. Choice D, "Because she wanted to find a red flower for herself," is incorrect because the Nightingale's intention was solely to find a red flower for the student, not for herself.

12. **D) Make a flower from music and her own heart's blood**

To create a red flower, the Nightingale had to make it from music and her own heart's blood. In the story, it is mentioned that the Nightingale approached a rosebush beneath the student's window and begged it for a red flower. The rosebush, unable to produce a red flower due to winter storms, revealed a secret way to create one. The Nightingale had to make the flower from music in the moonlight and color it with her own heart's blood. With great dedication and sacrifice, she pressed her chest against a thorn and sang all night long, infusing the flower with her lifeblood. This choice is correct because it accurately represents the method the Nightingale had to undertake to create the red flower.

The other choices are incorrect because they do not align with the actual process described in the story. Choice A, "Sing her sweetest song to a rosebush," is incorrect because although the Nightingale asked the rosebush for a red flower, singing her sweetest song was not the direct method of creating the flower. Choice B, "Exchange her feathers for a red flower," is incorrect because there is no mention of the Nightingale exchanging her feathers for a red flower. Choice C, "Ask the Chamberlain's nephew for a red flower," is incorrect because the Chamberlain's nephew is not involved in the Nightingale's quest to create a red flower.

13. C) He threw the flower into the street

When the student's beloved rejected the red flower, the student threw the flower into the street. In the story, it is mentioned that the student was heartbroken and angry at his beloved's lack of appreciation for the gift. Feeling rejected and disappointed, he reacted by discarding the flower he had received from the Nightingale. This choice is correct because it accurately represents the student's action in response to his beloved's rejection.

The other choices are incorrect because they do not align with the student's actual response in the story. Choice A, "He thanked her for her honesty," is incorrect because there is no mention of the student expressing gratitude towards his beloved for her honesty. Choice B, "He presented her with precious jewels," is incorrect because the student did not offer his beloved precious jewels after she rejected the red flower. Choice D, "He asked the Nightingale for another flower," is incorrect because the student did not seek another flower from the Nightingale after his beloved rejected the initial gift.

14. C) It had no effect as he was unaware of the sacrifice.

The Nightingale's sacrifice had no direct effect on the student because he was unaware of the Nightingale's selfless act. He remained ignorant of the pain and sacrifice she endured to create the red flower for him. Therefore, he did not have the opportunity to appreciate or understand the depth of her love and the significance of her sacrifice. The student's lack of awareness prevented him from experiencing any personal growth or change in his perception of love. While the Nightingale's sacrifice was profound and meaningful, it went unnoticed by the student, leaving him unaffected by its impact. The other choices are incorrect because they imply that the student had a specific reaction or change as a result of the Nightingale's sacrifice, which is not the case in this story.

15. B) He decided to give up on love.

After the student's beloved rejected the red flower he presented to her, he felt heartbroken and disappointed. He had made a sincere effort to fulfill her request, but it was not enough to win her affection. As a result, the student lost hope in love and became disenchanted with the idea of pursuing a romantic relationship. He felt hurt by his beloved's lack of appreciation and turned away from the magical world of love. The other choices are incorrect because they depict actions that the student did not take. He did not decide to become a dancer, find more red flowers, or write a love poem. Instead, he gave up on love altogether, choosing to retreat to his room and return to his dusty books, symbolizing his withdrawal from the realm of love and his decision to focus on other aspects of life.

16. C) Paragraph 9.

Paragraph 9 describes the Nightingale's sacrifice. It explains how the Nightingale accepted the challenge to create a red flower for the student. The Nightingale pressed her chest against a thorn and sang all night long, pouring her heart and soul into her song. Despite the increasing pain from the thorn, she persisted in singing about the birth of love and the essence of passion. The climax of her song coincided with the transformation of the flower on the rosebush, turning it from pale to deep red. Unfortunately, the Nightingale grew weaker and could no longer endure the piercing thorn. With her last breath, she was happy, knowing that the flower was complete. The other choices are incorrect because they do not describe the Nightingale's sacrifice. Paragraph 7 mentions the damaged rosebush revealing the secret to create a red flower, while Paragraphs 8 and 10 depict the student's actions and the outcome of his gift respectively.

17. **C) The student's dedication and passion for love.**

The red flower stained with the Nightingale's lifeblood symbolizes the student's dedication and passion for love. The Nightingale sacrificed her life to create the red flower, infusing it with her own heart's blood. This act represents the depth of the student's longing for love and his genuine devotion to his beloved. The flower serves as a tangible representation of the student's commitment and sincerity, as it was created through the Nightingale's sacrifice. It symbolizes the value of love and the profound impact it can have on a person's life. The other choices are incorrect because they do not accurately capture the symbolic meaning of the red flower. The student's wisdom and knowledge (choice A) are not directly related to the symbolism of the flower. The Chamberlain's nephew's precious jewels (choice B) represent material possessions, which contrast with the purity and selflessness of the Nightingale's sacrifice. The Nightingale's understanding of love (choice D) is reflected in her actions, but the symbol of the red flower primarily represents the student's dedication and passion for love.

A Devoted Friend

18. **C) Hans.**

The protagonist of the story is Hans. He is described as an honest and kind-hearted man who lives in a peaceful village. The story revolves around his experiences, actions, and perspective. The narrative focuses on Hans's friendship with the Miller and how he navigates the challenges and dynamics of their relationship. Throughout the story, we follow Hans's journey, including his contentment during favorable times, his struggles during winter, and his selfless acts of friendship towards the Miller. The other choices are incorrect because they do not accurately represent the main character of the story. Hugh (choice A) is mentioned as the Miller's name and is a friend of Hans, but he is not the central character or the focus of the narrative. The Miller (choice B) is a supporting character who interacts with Hans but does not drive the story. Therefore, the correct answer is C) Hans, as he is the main character and the story revolves around his experiences and actions.

19. **A) kindness, selflessness.**

In the given options, the words "kindness" and "selflessness" share the same suffix " -ness." The suffix "-ness" is used to form abstract nouns indicating a state or quality. In this case, both "kindness" and "selflessness" are abstract nouns formed by adding the suffix "-ness" to the base words "kind" and "selfless," respectively.

The other choices are incorrect because the words in those pairs do not have the same suffix. Choice B) "generous" and "happiness" do not share the same suffix. "Generous" is an adjective that does not have a suffix, while "happiness" has the suffix " -ness" attached to the adjective "happy." Choice C) "cottage" and "dilapidated" do not have the same suffix. "Cottage" is a noun without a suffix, while "dilapidated" is an adjective that does not have a suffix either. Choice D) "flowers" and "medicinal" do not have the same suffix. "Flowers" is a noun without a suffix, while "medicinal" is an adjective that does not have a suffix either.

20. **D) He believed people in trouble should be left alone.**

According to the story, the Miller stopped visiting Hans during the winter because he believed that people in trouble should be left alone. The Miller thought that seeing his warm home and abundant provisions might make Hans envious, so he chose to stay away during the difficult season. He believed that protecting Hans from temptations and preserving his contentment were acts of friendship. The Miller's actions reflected his belief that it was best to give Hans space and not interfere with his troubles. This choice is supported by paragraph 3 of the story, which states that the Miller claimed people in trouble should be left alone.

The other choices are incorrect because they do not accurately reflect the reason stated in the story. Choice A) states that the Miller became envious of Hans' garden, but there is no indication in the story that this is the case. Choice B) suggests that the Miller had fallen ill and could not leave his home, but there is no mention of illness in the story. Choice C) states that the Miller had moved to a different village, but there is no mention of him moving in the story.

21. **b) An old wheelbarrow.**

In the story, the Miller offered Hans an old wheelbarrow as a gift. The Miller believed in the importance of selflessness and true friendship, so he wanted to show his generosity to Hans. Even though the wheelbarrow was dilapidated and of lesser value compared to what Hans had intended to buy back, the Miller emphasized that true friendship involves acts of giving, regardless of the value of the gift. This choice is supported by paragraph 6 of the story, where the Miller offers his own dilapidated wheelbarrow to Hans as a gift in exchange for a basket of flowers.

The other choices are incorrect because they do not accurately represent what the Miller offered as a gift in the story. Choice a) suggests that the Miller offered Hans a bag of flour, but it was Hans who carried the heavy sack of flour to the market for the Miller in a later part of the story. Choice c) states that the Miller received a basket of flowers from Hans, but it was Hans who gave away all his precious primroses to the Miller, not the other way around. Choice d) suggests that the Miller offered Hans a dilapidated cottage, but there is no mention of the Miller giving Hans a cottage in the story.

22. **A) Sell them in the market.**

In the story, Hans intended to sell the flowers he grew in the market. During the winter, Hans faced hardships and suffered from cold and hunger. To overcome these challenges, he planned to sell the flowers he nurtured in his garden and use the earnings to buy back his wheelbarrow, which he had sold to survive the harsh season. This choice is supported by paragraph 5 of the story, where Hans expresses his plan to sell the flowers and buy back his wheelbarrow.

The other choices are incorrect because they do not accurately represent Hans's intention with the flowers he grew. Choice B) suggests that Hans intended to decorate his cottage with the flowers, but there is no mention of Hans using the flowers for decoration purposes. Choice C) states that Hans intended to give the flowers to the Miller's family, but there is no indication in the story that he had such intentions. Choice D) implies that Hans intended to use the flowers for medicinal purposes, but there is no mention of him using the flowers in this way.

23. **C) He did not want to appear unfriendly.**

Hans agreed to carry the Miller's sack of flour because he did not want to appear unfriendly. Despite being busy with his own chores, Hans reluctantly shouldered the heavy load and set off to the market, leaving behind his own tasks. He agreed to help the Miller because he valued their friendship and did not want to give the impression that he was unwilling to assist. This choice is supported by paragraph 8 of the story, where it is mentioned that Hans reluctantly agrees to carry the heavy sack of flour, not wanting to appear unfriendly.

The other choices are incorrect because they do not accurately explain Hans's motivation for agreeing to carry the sack of flour. Choice A) suggests that Hans wanted to impress the Miller, but there is no indication in the story that this was his intention. Choice B) states that Hans had nothing better to do, but the story does not mention his lack of other tasks or responsibilities. Choice D) implies that Hans needed the exercise, but there is no indication that this was his reason for accepting the task.

24. **A) He was grateful and appreciative.**

Hans felt grateful and appreciative towards the Miller's acts of friendship. Throughout the story, it is evident that Hans values their friendship and holds the Miller in high regard. When the Miller finally visits him after winter, Hans gratefully expresses his happiness and shares his plan to sell the flowers and buy back his wheelbarrow. Additionally, when the Miller offers his dilapidated wheelbarrow as a gift, Hans gladly accepts it, valuing the Miller's friendship more than material possessions. These instances demonstrate Hans's genuine appreciation for the Miller's gestures of kindness and support.

The other choices are incorrect because they do not accurately reflect Hans's feelings towards the Miller's acts of friendship. Choice B) suggests that Hans was suspicious and doubtful, but there is no indication in the story that he had any doubts or suspicions about the Miller's intentions. Choice C) states that Hans was envious and resentful, but the story portrays Hans as a kind-hearted and grateful individual who does not harbor such negative emotions. Choice D) implies that Hans was indifferent and uninterested, but this contradicts his actions and the gratitude he expresses towards the Miller.

25. **C) The Miller's friendship.**

Hans valued the Miller's friendship more than material possessions. Throughout the story, Hans demonstrates his deep appreciation for the Miller's acts of kindness and support. When the Miller offers his dilapidated wheelbarrow as a gift, Hans gladly accepts it, prioritizing their friendship over the value of the gift itself. Additionally, when the Miller requests Hans to carry a heavy sack of flour to the market, Hans agrees, not wanting to appear unfriendly despite being busy with his own tasks. These actions illustrate that Hans places a higher importance on maintaining a strong bond of friendship with the Miller than on acquiring material wealth or possessions.

The other choices are incorrect because they do not accurately reflect what Hans values. Choice A) suggests that Hans values money and wealth, but there is no indication in the story that he prioritizes material wealth over friendship. Choice B) states that Hans values status and reputation, but there is no evidence to support this claim in the story. Hans's actions and attitudes are driven by his genuine care and appreciation for the Miller, not by a desire for social standing or reputation. Choice D) implies that Hans values personal happiness and well-being above all else, but while Hans does seek happiness, his actions demonstrate that he values his friendship with the Miller as an important aspect of his overall happiness and well-being.

The Wonderful World of Kaleidoscopes

26. **B) An optical device.**

According to the passage, a kaleidoscope is described as a fascinating optical device. It consists of a tube with mirrors and colored glass or beads inside. When you look through the eyepiece and rotate the tube, you can see ever-changing patterns and colors. The passage explains how the mirrors inside the kaleidoscope create multiple reflections of the objects inside, resulting in stunning patterns. It also mentions that kaleidoscopes are enjoyed by people of all ages and have both entertainment and educational value. While kaleidoscopes can be used as toys, decorative pieces, or even have rotating mechanisms, the primary definition and purpose of a kaleidoscope, as stated in the passage, is as an optical device that creates beautiful patterns through the reflection of light and the use of mirrors.

The other choices are incorrect because they do not accurately describe the primary function and purpose of a kaleidoscope, as stated in the passage. Choice A) suggests that a kaleidoscope is primarily an educational toy, but while it does have educational value, it is not solely defined as a toy. Choice C) states that a kaleidoscope is a decorative piece, but while kaleidoscopes can be displayed as decorative items, they serve a functional purpose as an optical device. Choice D) describes a rotating mechanism, but while some modern kaleidoscopes may have rotating mechanisms, it is not the defining characteristic of a kaleidoscope.

27. **C) By explaining the principles of optics.**

In paragraph 3, the author helps the reader understand the mechanism of a kaleidoscope by explaining the principles of optics. The passage mentions that the magic of a kaleidoscope lies in its mirrors, which are placed at specific angles inside the tube. The author then goes on to explain that these mirrors reflect and multiply the images, creating the stunning patterns we see. This explanation of how the mirrors work to create reflections and patterns helps the reader understand the mechanism of a kaleidoscope.

The other choices are incorrect because they do not accurately describe how the author helps the reader understand the mechanism of a kaleidoscope in paragraph 3. Choice A) suggests that the author quotes inventors, but there are no quotations from inventors in the paragraph. Choice B) mentions describing the materials used, but while the passage mentions colored glass or beads inside the kaleidoscope, it does not focus on the materials as a means of understanding the mechanism. Choice D) refers to historical anecdotes, but paragraph 3 does not provide historical anecdotes; it focuses on explaining the working principles of a kaleidoscope.

28. **B) Greek.**

According to paragraph 2, the word "kaleidoscope" comes from Greek words meaning "beautiful form to see." The passage mentions that the patterns created by a kaleidoscope are truly beautiful, and the Greek origin of the word reflects the concept of beauty. By providing this information, the passage explains that the word "kaleidoscope" has its roots in the Greek language.

The other choices are incorrect because they do not align with the information provided in the passage. Choice A) suggests that the origin is Latin, but the passage explicitly states that the word comes from Greek. Choice C) mentions French, which is not mentioned in the passage as the origin of the word. Choice D) refers to English, but the passage does not indicate that the word "kaleidoscope" originated in the English language.

29. **A) They reflect and multiply the images.**

According to paragraph 3, the mirrors inside a kaleidoscope play a crucial role in creating the patterns. The passage explains that these mirrors are placed at specific angles inside the tube. When the tube is rotated, the mirrors reflect and multiply the images of the colored glass or beads inside the kaleidoscope. This reflection and multiplication of images create the stunning and ever-changing patterns that we see when looking through the kaleidoscope's eyepiece.

The other choices are incorrect because they do not align with the information provided in the passage. Choice B) suggests that the mirrors rotate to create new shapes, but the passage does not mention any rotation of the mirrors themselves. It is the rotation of the entire tube that causes the mirrors to reflect and multiply the images. Choice C) mentions enhancing the visual experience, which is not the specific function of the mirrors inside the kaleidoscope. Choice D) refers to refraction of light, but the passage focuses on the role of mirrors in creating the patterns, not the refraction of light.

30. **A) Developing spatial awareness.**

According to paragraph 5, one of the educational benefits of using a kaleidoscope is developing spatial awareness. By observing the patterns formed in a kaleidoscope, individuals can enhance their understanding of space and how objects relate to one another. As they rotate the tube and witness the changing patterns, they gain a sense of the arrangement and positioning of the reflected images. This helps in developing spatial perception and recognizing patterns in the surrounding environment.

The other choices are incorrect because they do not align with the information provided in the passage. Choice B) suggests that using a kaleidoscope enhances artistic skills, but the passage does not specifically mention this benefit. While individuals may appreciate the artistic qualities of the patterns, the passage primarily focuses on the visual experience rather than artistic skill development. Choice C) regarding memory retention is not mentioned in the passage as an educational benefit of using a kaleidoscope. The passage emphasizes the visual and experiential aspects of a kaleidoscope rather than memory-related benefits. Choice D) suggesting physical exercise is not mentioned in the passage. Using a kaleidoscope does not involve physical activity or stimulation of physical exercise.

31. **D) People of all ages.**

According to paragraph 4, kaleidoscopes have been enjoyed by people of all ages. They provide a source of endless entertainment and inspiration. Children are often captivated by the kaleidoscope's ever-changing patterns, while adults appreciate its artistic and meditative qualities. This suggests that kaleidoscopes are not limited to a specific age group and can be enjoyed by everyone, regardless of their age.

The other choices are incorrect because they do not encompass the full range of individuals who can enjoy kaleidoscopes. Choice A) stating only children can enjoy kaleidoscopes is incorrect as the passage mentions that adults also appreciate their qualities. Choice B) suggesting only adults can enjoy kaleidoscopes is incorrect because children are explicitly mentioned as being captivated by the patterns. Choice C) limiting the enjoyment to artists and collectors is incorrect as the passage does not mention this specific group but rather focuses on the broader appeal to people of all ages.

32. **A) They have rotating mechanisms.**

According to paragraph 6, modern kaleidoscopes come in various forms. While traditional handheld kaleidoscopes are still popular, modern kaleidoscopes can be larger and mounted on a stand or even displayed as decorative pieces. What sets modern kaleidoscopes apart is that some of them are equipped with rotating mechanisms. This means that instead of manually rotating the tube, these kaleidoscopes have mechanisms that allow for automatic rotation, enhancing the visual experience.

The other choices are incorrect because they do not accurately describe the difference between modern and traditional kaleidoscopes. Choice B) suggesting they are made of different materials is incorrect because the passage does not mention a distinction in materials. Choice C) stating they produce sound effects is incorrect as the passage does not mention any sound effects associated with kaleidoscopes. Choice D) suggesting they have built-in cameras is incorrect because there is no mention of cameras in the passage.

33. **D) The beauty and enjoyment of kaleidoscopes.**

The main idea of the passage is to highlight the beauty and enjoyment that kaleidoscopes bring to people. The passage describes kaleidoscopes as fascinating optical devices that have captured the imagination of people for centuries. It goes on to explain how kaleidoscopes create mesmerizing patterns and colors through the reflection of mirrors and the use of colored glass or beads. The passage also emphasizes that kaleidoscopes provide a source of endless entertainment and inspiration for people of all ages. It mentions how children are captivated by the ever-changing patterns and how adults appreciate their artistic and meditative qualities. Furthermore, the passage mentions that kaleidoscopes have educational value, helping develop skills such as color sense, pattern recognition, and spatial awareness. However, the main focus of the passage is on the beauty and enjoyment of kaleidoscopes, making option D the correct choice.

The other choices are incorrect because they do not accurately represent the main idea of the passage. Option A) suggesting the history of kaleidoscopes is incorrect because while the passage mentions the fascination with kaleidoscopes throughout history, it is not the main focus. Option B) suggesting the different types of kaleidoscopes is incorrect because while the passage mentions various forms of kaleidoscopes, it is not the central idea. Option C) suggesting the educational value of kaleidoscopes is incorrect because while the passage mentions their educational benefits, it is not the main idea being conveyed.

The Magical Adventures of Toylandia

34. A) Paragraph 1.

The paragraph that introduces the magical world of Toylandia is Paragraph 1. In this paragraph, it is mentioned that Toylandia is a magical world where a wondrous transformation occurs when the moon bathes the land in its ethereal glow. It describes how toys come to life at midnight, eager to embark on enchanting adventures. This paragraph sets the stage for the magical world and captures the readers' attention by introducing the concept of toys coming alive in Toylandia.

The other choices are incorrect because they do not accurately represent the paragraph where the magical world of Toylandia is introduced. Option B) Paragraph 2 describes the whimsical realm of Toylandia, with sparkling cobblestones and toys engaging in various activities. Option C) Paragraph 3 introduces the grand toy castle and the Toy King and Queen who care for lost toys. Option D) Paragraph 4 introduces the character of Jasper, the little wooden puppet, and his wish to find a special purpose.

35. D) Their toy boxes.

According to paragraph 7 of the story, when dawn approaches, the toys in Toylandia return to their still forms and await the next moonlit adventure. This implies that they go back to their original state and return to their respective toy boxes. The passage mentions that Toylandia is a secret world hidden from grown-up eyes, and the toys come to life only during moonlit nights. Therefore, when daylight comes, the toys go back to their toy boxes to appear as ordinary playthings. This choice is supported by the information provided in the passage.

The other choices are incorrect because they do not align with the information given in the passage. Option A) Toylandia Castle is mentioned in paragraph 3 as the grand toy castle where the Toy King and Queen reign, but it is not specified that the toys go there when dawn approaches. Option B) The meadows of candy-colored flowers are mentioned in paragraph 2 as a location where toy animals frolic, but it is not stated that the toys go there when dawn arrives. Option C) While the toys bring joy and magic to children's lives, there is no indication in the passage that they go to children's homes when dawn approaches.

36. C) They could communicate and empathize with children.

According to paragraph 3 of the story, each toy in Toylandia possesses its own unique magic, which grants it the ability to communicate and empathize with children. This implies that toys have the special power to understand and connect with children on an emotional level. In paragraph 6, it is mentioned that Jasper discovered the true meaning of friendship and the power of imagination in Toylandia, suggesting that he realized the toys' ability to communicate and empathize. This choice is directly supported by the information provided in the passage.

The other choices are incorrect because they do not align with the information given in the passage: Option A) Flying is not mentioned or implied in the story. Option B) The power of invisibility is not mentioned or implied in the story. Option D) While Jasper's wish was granted to be transported to Toylandia, there is no indication in the passage that toys have the power to grant wishes.

37. C) Paragraph 3.

In paragraph 3 of the story, it is described that at the heart of Toylandia stood a grand toy castle, where the Toy King and Queen reigned with benevolence. The passage further states that the castle served as a sanctuary for lost toys, providing them with love, care, and a sense of belonging. This information clearly identifies the Toylandia castle as a place where lost toys find refuge and are given the support they need. Therefore, paragraph 3 is the correct choice.

The other choices are incorrect because they do not describe the Toylandia castle as a sanctuary for lost toys: Option A) Paragraph 1 introduces the magical world of Toylandia and the transformation of toys when the moon bathes the land, but it does not mention the castle or its purpose. Option B) Paragraph 2 describes the whimsical realm of Toylandia, but it does not specifically mention the castle as a sanctuary for lost toys. Option D) Paragraph 4 introduces the character of Jasper, a wooden puppet, and his wish to have a special purpose, but it does not discuss the castle or its role as a sanctuary for lost toys.

38. B) Mr. Barnaby and Coco.

In paragraph 5 of the story, it is mentioned that Jasper, the wooden puppet, made friends with a mischievous wind-up monkey named Coco and a wise old teddy bear named Mr. Barnaby. This information clearly states that Coco and Mr. Barnaby were Jasper's friends in Toylandia. Therefore, option B is the correct answer.

The other choices are incorrect because they do not accurately represent Jasper's friends: Option A) Coco and Teddy: This choice is incorrect because Teddy is not mentioned as one of Jasper's friends. Instead, it is Mr. Barnaby who is mentioned. Option C) Teddy and Mr. Barnaby: This choice is incorrect because it switches the names of Jasper's friends. It was Coco and not Teddy who became friends with Jasper. Option D) Coco and Jasper: This choice is incorrect because it only mentions Coco and Jasper, leaving out Mr. Barnaby, who was also mentioned as one of Jasper's friends.

39. B) Imagination can transform the ordinary into the extraordinary.

The main message of the story is about the power of imagination and how it can transform ordinary objects, in this case, toys, into something extraordinary. Throughout the story, Toylandia is described as a magical world where toys come to life and embark on enchanting adventures. The story highlights how toys have the ability to ignite dreams, spark creativity, and bring joy to children's lives. It emphasizes that toys are more than just ordinary playthings; they become cherished companions and bridges between the real world and the realm of endless possibilities. This message encourages readers to embrace their imagination and recognize the potential for magic and wonder in everyday objects. Therefore, option B is the correct answer.

The other choices are incorrect because they do not accurately reflect the main message of the story: Option A) Toys are just ordinary playthings: This choice contradicts the story's emphasis on the magical transformation of toys and the role they play in bringing joy and happiness. Option C) Adults should never enter Toylandia: This choice is not mentioned or implied in the story. There is no indication that adults entering Toylandia is a concern or part of the main message. Option D) Toys should only be played with during the day: This choice is not a central theme in the story. While it mentions the toys returning to their still forms at dawn, it does not convey the main message of the story about the power of imagination.

40. C) Return to their original toy forms and await the next moonlit adventure.

At the end of the story, the passage states that as dawn approaches, the toys in Toylandia return to their still forms, awaiting the next moonlit adventure. This implies that the toys will go back to their original toy forms, becoming inanimate objects again. They will rest until the next night when the moon bathes Toylandia in its ethereal glow, at which point they will awaken and come to life once more, ready to embark on new enchanting adventures. This choice aligns with the information provided in the passage and suggests that the toys in Toylandia have a cycle of transformation, where they alternate between being alive during the night and returning to their toy forms during the day.

The other choices are incorrect because they are not supported by the information in the passage: Option A) Have a tea party with the Toy King and Queen: While the Toy King and Queen are mentioned in the story, there is no specific mention of the toys having a tea party with them at the end. Option B) Transform into real-life animals and explore the world: The passage does not mention the toys transforming into real-life animals or venturing beyond the confines of Toylandia. Their adventures are described within the boundaries of the magical world. Option D) Build a new toy castle in a different part of Toylandia: The passage does not mention the toys building a new toy castle or changing their location within Toylandia. The focus is on their transformation and awaiting their next adventure.

41. B) "A Magical Night in Toylandia."

The alternative title "A Magical Night in Toylandia" reflects the main theme and setting of the story. It highlights the magical aspect of the world of Toylandia and sets the stage for the enchanting adventures that take place during the night when the toys come to life. This title captures the essence of the story, emphasizing the magical transformation and the whimsical nature of the toy characters. It suggests that readers will be taken on a journey through a magical and captivating world.

The other choices are incorrect because they do not accurately capture the main focus or theme of the story: Option A) "The Adventures of Jasper on the flight": This title focuses solely on the character of Jasper and suggests a different storyline involving flying, which is not a prominent element in the original story. Option C) "The Enchanted World of Humans": This title suggests a different perspective where the story revolves around the enchanted world of humans, which is not the main focus of the original story. Option D) "Exploring Toys": This title focuses on the general concept of exploring toys, which does not capture the specific magical and imaginative world of Toylandia presented in the story.

Emily And Grandpa's Enchanting Journey Through Nature

42. C) Country roads.

Emily and her grandfather went for a walk along the country roads. The passage mentions that Emily asks her grandfather if they can go for a walk through the country roads, and her grandfather agrees, suggesting that they explore the wonders of nature together. Throughout the story, they encounter various natural elements like butterflies, fish, squirrels, birds, and an old oak tree, which indicates that they were immersed in a natural outdoor setting. The description of rolling hills, green meadows, and the scent of wildflowers further supports the idea that they were exploring the countryside. Therefore, the answer choice C) Country roads is the correct one.

The other choices are incorrect because they do not match the information provided in the passage: Option A) City streets: The passage does not mention anything about Emily and her grandfather walking through city streets. On the contrary, the emphasis is on the countryside and nature. Option B) Beach: The passage does not mention any indication of a beach setting. The focus is on the countryside with rolling hills and meadows. Option D) Forest: While the passage mentions trees, it does not specify that Emily and her grandfather walked through a forest. The mention of country roads suggests a more open landscape rather than a dense forest setting.

43. C) Fish.

Near the babbling brook, Emily found fish swimming among the pebbles. The passage describes how Emily kneels down by the water and becomes mesmerized by the sight of tiny fish swimming in the brook. Emily then asks her grandfather why the fish swim together in groups. This indicates that they encountered fish near the babbling brook during their walk. Therefore, the answer choice C) Fish is the correct one.

The other choices are incorrect because they do not match the information provided in the passage: Option A) Butterflies: While butterflies are mentioned earlier in the story, they are not specifically associated with the babbling brook scene. Emily's question about butterflies occurs before they reach the brook. Option B) Squirrels: Squirrels are mentioned later in the passage, but they are not associated with the babbling brook.

Squirrels are spotted scampering up trees, not near the water. Option D) Birds: Birds are mentioned later in the passage, but they are not specifically associated with the babbling brook scene. Birds are mentioned as building nests and are spotted in various parts of their walk, but there is no mention of birds near the brook.

44. C) to attract attention

The purpose of the butterflies' colorful wings is to attract attention. In the passage, Grandpa Thomas explains to Emily that the bright colors on a butterfly's wings are like a work of art and are specifically designed to attract our attention. This helps the butterflies stand out in the world and catch the eyes of others. The vibrant colors of their wings serve as a way for butterflies to communicate and be noticed. This helps in various aspects of their lives, such as finding mates and ensuring their survival. Therefore, the answer choice C) To attract attention is the correct one.

The other choices are incorrect because they do not align with the information provided in the passage: Option A) To blend in with their surroundings: The passage does not mention anything about butterflies needing to blend in with their surroundings. On the contrary, their bright colors are intended to make them noticeable. Option B) To scare away predators: There is no mention in the passage of butterflies using their colorful wings to scare away predators. Instead, their colors serve a different purpose of attracting attention. Option D) To keep them warm: The passage does not indicate that the colorful wings of butterflies help in keeping them warm. Their wings serve different functions related to communication and attracting attention.

45. B) To find food more easily

Fish swim together in groups, called schools, to find food more easily. In the passage, when Emily asks her grandfather why fish swim together in groups, Grandpa Thomas explains that fish swim in schools for protection and to find food more easily. Swimming in a group allows them to watch out for each other and increases their chances of finding food. By staying together, the fish create a collective presence that can intimidate predators and reduce the likelihood of an individual fish being targeted. Therefore, the answer choice B) To find food more easily is the correct one.

The other choices are incorrect because they do not align with the information provided in the passage: Option A) For mating purposes: The passage does not mention anything about fish swimming together in groups specifically for mating purposes. The focus is on finding food and protection. Option C) To escape from predators: While swimming in groups can provide some level of protection against predators, the primary reason mentioned in the passage is to find food more easily, not to escape from predators. Option D) To sleep together: The passage does not mention anything about fish swimming together in groups, specifically to sleep together. The emphasis is on their collective behavior for finding food and protection.

46. C) Oaktree

Emily and her grandfather came across an oak tree during their walk. In the passage, Emily notices an old oak tree with gnarled branches and wonders if it has a story to tell. The description of the tree as an "old oak tree" indicates that it belongs to the oak tree species. Therefore, the answer choice C) Oak tree is the correct one.

The other choices are incorrect because they do not align with the information provided in the passage: Option A) Pine tree: The passage does not mention anything about a pine tree. The focus is on the oak tree that Emily and her grandfather encounter. Option B) Maple tree: The passage does not mention anything about a maple tree. The specific tree mentioned is an oak tree, not a maple tree. Option D) Willow tree: The passage does not mention anything about a willow tree. The focus is on the oak tree that Emily and her grandfather come across.

47. C) They listen to its stories

Emily and her grandfather sit under the shade of the old tree when they come across it. In the passage, Emily wonders if the tree has a story to tell, and her grandfather mentions that if the tree could speak, it would tell them tales of the past. The description of Emily and her grandfather leaning against the tree and Emily expressing her love for her grandfather's stories indicates that they sit under the tree to listen to its stories. Therefore, the answer choice C) They listen to its stories is the correct one.

The other choices are incorrect because they do not align with the information provided in the passage: Option A) They climb it: The passage does not mention anything about Emily and her grandfather climbing the tree. The focus is on them sitting under its shade. Option B) They sit under its shade: This is the correct answer choice, as explained above. Option D) They take pictures of it: The passage does not mention anything about Emily and her grandfather taking pictures of the tree. The focus is on them appreciating the tree's stories and the bond between Emily and her grandfather.

48. C) Fascinated

In the context of the story, the word "mesmerized" means fascinated. When Emily sees the tiny fish swimming among the pebbles in the babbling brook, she becomes captivated by their movements and is filled with a sense of wonder. The word "mesmerized" is used to describe the intense fascination and enchantment Emily experiences as she watches the fish. Therefore, the correct answer is C) Fascinated.

The other choices are incorrect because they do not accurately convey the meaning of "mesmerized" in the context of the story: Option A) Frightened: The word "mesmerized" does not indicate fear or being frightened. Instead, it implies being deeply engaged and captivated. Option B) Bored: The word "mesmerized" suggests the opposite of being bored. It describes a state of intense interest and fascination. Option D) Confused: While "mesmerized" can sometimes be associated with a state of confusion, in this context, it specifically refers to being fascinated and engrossed by the sight of the fish in the brook.

49. D) "The school of fish moved in perfect synchronization,"

In the given options, the sentence that uses the word "school" with its primary meaning is D) "The school of fish moved in perfect synchronization." In this sentence, the word "school" refers to a group of fish swimming together, which is the primary meaning of the word.

The other choices are incorrect because they use the word "school" in different contexts and with different meanings: Option A) "She has completed her schooling last year" uses "schooling" to refer to the process of education or attending school, rather than a group of fish. Option B) "The old building had been transformed into a school of art" uses "school" to refer to a place of learning or institution, in this case, a school of art. Option C) "She schooled herself in various subjects to broaden her knowledge" uses "schooled" as a verb to mean educating or teaching oneself, rather than referring to a group of fish.

50. **A) "A Walk in the Countryside"**

The most suitable alternative title for Emily's story would be A) "A Walk in the Countryside." This title captures the central theme of the story, which is Emily and her grandfather's journey through nature. It emphasizes the adventure they have while exploring the countryside and highlights the connection they share with the natural world. The title also reflects the sense of wonder and enchantment that Emily experiences during their walk.

The other choices are incorrect because they do not fully encompass the essence of the story: B) "Emily and Her Grandfather" focuses only on the characters involved and does not capture the nature-centric aspect of the story. C) "Grandpa Thomas" highlights one character specifically and does not give a sense of the overall narrative or setting. D) "The Curious Little Girl and the Country Roads" focuses primarily on Emily and the country roads, but does not encompass the broader theme of their enchanting journey through nature.

Grade 5
Ans keys

THE GENERAL AND THE FOX

1. **A) A deep and narrow rocky abyss**

Explanation:

The picture that best represents the chasm in the rocks where Aristomenes was thrown is A) A deep and narrow rocky abyss. The passage describes the chasm as a "narrow chasm or hole in the rocks" that was "very deep" and had "rocky walls surrounded him on every side." This option accurately portrays the description of a deep and narrow rocky chasm.

The other choices are incorrect because they do not match the description provided in the passage. B) A vast open field does not align with the description of a chasm in the rocks. C) A serene mountain peak does not capture the concept of a narrow and deep chasm. D) A dense forest is also not consistent with the rocky chasm described in the story. Therefore, option A) is the most suitable representation of the chasm where Aristomenes was thrown based on the provided details.

2. **B) Ran quickly and playfully.**

Explanation:

The word "scampered" means to run quickly and playfully. In the context of the passage, when Aristomenes sees the large fox coming towards him, he waits quietly and then suddenly springs up and seizes it by the tail. The word "scampered" indicates that the fox reacted to being grabbed by running away as fast as it could. The description of the fox running quickly and playfully aligns with the meaning of the word "scampered."

The other options are incorrect. A) Moved stealthily and quietly does not fit the behavior of the fox in the passage. C) Climbed with great effort is not applicable since the fox is described as running rather than climbing. D) Crawled slowly and cautiously also does not match the energetic and quick movement of the fox. Therefore, option B) is the correct interpretation of the word "scampered" in the given context.

3. **A) He was captured and taken prisoner.**

Explanation:

In the battle with the Spartans, the Greek general Aristomenes faced defeat. According to the passage, his army was beaten, and as a result, he was taken prisoner by the Spartans. This is stated in the sentence: "Once, however, in a great battle with the Spartans, his army was beaten and he was taken prisoner." Therefore, option A) He was captured and taken prisoner is the correct description of what happened to Aristomenes in the battle with the Spartans.

Grade 5
Ans keys

The other options are incorrect. B) He led his army to victory contradicts the information provided in the passage about his army being beaten. C) He escaped unharmed from the battle is not supported by the passage as it specifically mentions that he was taken prisoner. D) He was wounded but survived the battle does not have any mention of him being

wounded or his survival. Therefore, option A) is the correct answer based on the information provided in the passage.

4. **C) They intended to throw him into a deep chasm.**

Explanation:

The Spartans, upon capturing Aristomenes, planned to deal with him by throwing him into a deep chasm. In the passage, it is mentioned that the Spartans said to one another, "Let us throw this fellow into the rocky chasm. Then we may be sure that he will never trouble us again." They saw the chasm as a place to dispose of their enemies, and this was their intended course of action for Aristomenes. Therefore, option C) They intended to throw him into a deep chasm accurately reflects the Spartans' plan for dealing with Aristomenes after capturing him.

The other options are incorrect. A) They wanted to negotiate a peace treaty with him is not supported by the passage, as it describes the Spartans' hatred towards Aristomenes and their desire to destroy him. B) They admired his bravery and decided to release him is not mentioned in the passage either. D) They planned to offer him a high-ranking position in their army is not suggested or implied in the passage. Hence, option C) is the correct answer based on the information provided.

5. **D) He fell onto bushes and vines.**

Explanation:

Aristomenes managed to survive after being thrown into the chasm by falling onto bushes and vines. While there were speculations among some Greeks that an eagle might have saved him, the passage states that it is not likely. The narrator suggests that Aristomenes most likely fell onto some bushes and vines that grew in certain parts of the chasm, which helped cushion his fall and prevent serious injury. Therefore, option D) He fell onto bushes and vines is the correct explanation of how Aristomenes survived the fall into the chasm, based on the information provided in the passage.

The other options are incorrect. A) An eagle carried him to safety is mentioned as speculation but dismissed as unlikely. B) He was rescued by a group of Greeks is not supported by the passage. C) He found a hidden tunnel is not mentioned or suggested in the passage. Thus, option D) is the best answer based on the details given.

6. **C) A fox that came towards him.**

Explanation:

Aristomenes discovered a narrow passageway out of the chasm because a fox came towards him. In the passage, it is mentioned that Aristomenes was startled by a noise close to him and saw something moving

Grade 5

Ans keys

among the rocks at the bottom of the chasm. He watched quietly and observed a large fox coming towards him. This event led to his discovery of the narrow passageway as he followed the frightened fox, clinging to its tail. The fox ran into a narrow cleft and through a long, dark passage, which Aristomenes then traversed. Therefore, option C) A fox that came towards him accurately describes what led Aristomenes to discover the narrow passageway out of the chasm.

The other options are incorrect. A) A sound of movement among the rocks is a general description of the noise Aristomenes heard but does not specifically indicate how he discovered the passageway. B) A ray of light shining from above is mentioned later in the passage as what Aristomenes saw after he held onto the fox and reached the narrow passage's entrance. D) A group of Spartans searching for him is not mentioned or suggested in the passage as being the cause of Aristomenes' discovery of the passageway. Hence, option C) is the correct answer based on the information provided.

7. **B) By following the fox through a narrow passage.**

Explanation:

Aristomenes eventually escaped from the chasm by following the fox through a narrow passage. In the passage, it is described how Aristomenes seized the fox by its tail and the frightened animal ran away, with Aristomenes clinging to it. The fox led him into a narrow cleft and through a long, dark passage that was barely large enough for a man's body. Aristomenes held on and eventually saw a ray of light, which was the sunlight streaming in at the entrance to the passage. Although the way became too narrow for his body to pass through, he let go of the fox, allowing it to run out, and then began widening the passageway himself by loosening the rocks. With great labor, he managed to create enough space to squeeze through and eventually emerged into the open air. Therefore, option B) By following the fox through a narrow passage is the correct explanation of how Aristomenes escaped from the chasm.

The other options are incorrect. A) By climbing up the rocky walls is not mentioned or suggested in the passage as a means of escape. C) By calling for help until someone found him is not described in the passage, and there is no indication of anyone finding Aristomenes in the chasm. D) By digging a new pathway with his bare hands is not mentioned or implied in the passage. Hence, option B) is the accurate answer based on the details provided.

8. **A) The power of perseverance and determination.**

Explanation:

The sentence that best states the theme of this story is A) The power of perseverance and determination. Throughout the story, Aristomenes faces numerous challenges and obstacles, from being captured by the Spartans and thrown into a deep chasm to enduring hunger, thirst, and the dim light of his prison. Despite these hardships, Aristomenes does not give up. He remains determined to find a way to escape and continues to persevere even in the face of seemingly impossible odds. His encounter with the fox and his resourcefulness in widening the passageway demonstrate his determination and resolve. The theme of the story revolves around the idea that with perseverance and determination, one can overcome even the most challenging circumstances.

The other options are not the central theme of the story. B) The importance of being kind to one's enemies is not the primary focus of the narrative; rather, it portrays the cruelty of war and the lack of kindness towards enemies during that time. C) The bravery and wisdom of Aristomenes is an aspect of his character but does not encompass the central theme explored in the story. D) The savagery and cruelty of war is touched upon in the story but is not the overarching theme. Hence, option A) is the correct answer based on the main message conveyed in the narrative.

Mrs. Spring Fragrance

9. C) She considers it beautiful and important.

According to the passage, Mrs. Spring Fragrance's opinion of the American language is that she considers it beautiful and important. The passage tells us that when Mrs. Spring Fragrance arrived in Seattle, she didn't know any American words. However, after five years, she had learned so many American words that her husband and everyone who knew her believed there were no more American words for her to learn. This shows that Mrs. Spring Fragrance put in effort and dedication to learn the American language. The other choices are incorrect because the passage doesn't suggest that Mrs. Spring Fragrance finds the American language challenging to learn (choice A). It also doesn't indicate that she believes it is unnecessary to learn (choice B). Additionally, there is no mention of her thinking the American language is inferior to the Chinese language (choice D). The passage mainly focuses on Mrs. Spring Fragrance's successful acquisition of American words, leading to the conclusion that she considers the American language beautiful and important.

10. B) "Stopping by the woods"

According to the passage, the American poem mentioned by Mrs. Spring Fragrance is B) "Stopping by the woods." Mrs. Spring Fragrance comforted Laura by sharing lines from this poem, which are: "The woods are lovely, dark and deep, But I have promises to keep, And miles to go before I sleep, And miles to go before I sleep." The poem's title is "Stopping by the woods on a snowy evening."

The other options are incorrect. A) "Drink to me only with thine eyes" is not mentioned in the passage and is actually a line from a poem by Ben Jonson, not an American poem. C) "To be, or not to be" is a famous soliloquy from Shakespeare's play Hamlet, not an American poem. D) "The Raven" is a renowned poem written by Edgar Allan Poe, but it is not mentioned in the passage. Therefore, the correct answer is B) "Stopping by the woods," as it is the only poem mentioned in the given passage.

11. A) Familiar with American customs and culture

In paragraph 2, the word "Americanized" most likely means A) Familiar with American customs and culture. The passage mentions that Mr. Spring Fragrance, also known as Sing Yook, was Chinese but had become "Americanized." This implies that he has adapted to and assimilated American customs and culture to some extent. The term "Americanized" commonly refers to the process of adopting or becoming familiar with the customs, practices, and way of life in America. The other options are not the most suitable interpretations in the given context. B) Born and raised in America is not explicitly stated in the passage. C) Having American ancestry and D) Traveling frequently to America are not directly related to the meaning of "Americanized" as described in the passage. Therefore, option A) is the most appropriate interpretation based on the information provided.

12. **D) Mrs. Spring Fragrance had learned all the American words**

When Mr. Spring Fragrance said, "There are no more American words for her learning," he meant that D) Mrs. Spring Fragrance had learned all the American words. The statement suggests that Mrs. Spring Fragrance has reached a point where she has acquired a comprehensive knowledge of the American language, and there are no further American words left for her to learn. This indicates that she has already mastered a significant vocabulary and is well-versed in American words and expressions. The other options do not align with the meaning of the statement. B) Mrs. Spring Fragrance couldn't learn any more American words contradicts the idea that she had successfully acquired a wide range of American words. C) Mrs. Spring Fragrance had forgotten the American words she learned implies a loss of knowledge, which is not indicated in the statement. A) Mrs. Spring Fragrance was still learning American words conflicts with the understanding that she had completed her learning and there were no more words left for her to acquire. Therefore, option D) best reflects the intended meaning based on the given statement.

13. **C) being a talented baseball player.**

The passage mentions that Kai Tzu, who was born in America, had gained recognition as one of the best pitchers on the Coast. This indicates that he excelled in the sport of baseball and was known for his skills and talent in that particular field. The other options are not supported by the information provided in the passage. A) Singing American songs and B) playing the piano are not mentioned as Kai Tzu's talents or areas of expertise. D) Writing poetry is also not attributed to Kai Tzu in the passage. Therefore, option C) accurately describes what Kai Tzu was known for based on the given information.

14. **A) talking about a beautiful walk.**

In the passage, it is mentioned that Mrs. Spring Fragrance described the beautiful daffodils in the green grass and the fragrance of the wallflower during her walk. She shared this experience with Laura in an attempt to uplift her spirits. The other options are not supported by the information provided. B) Giving her a gift, C) playing the piano, and D) taking her to a baseball game are not mentioned as methods used by Mrs. Spring Fragrance to cheer up Laura. Therefore, option A) is the correct choice based on the given details.

15. **D) He repeated the lines of the poem.**

Explanation: According to the passage, Mr. Spring Fragrance responded to the American poem by repeating its lines. This shows that he paid attention to the poem and remembered its words. The passage does not provide information about whether Mr. Spring Fragrance agreed or disagreed with the message of the poem, or if he understood its meaning. It only states that he repeated the lines. This suggests that Mr. Spring Fragrance was interested in the poem and wanted to recall its words. Therefore, the correct answer is D) He repeated the lines of the poem.

The other choices are incorrect because the passage does not support them. A) He agreed with the message of the poem is not mentioned in the passage. B) He disagreed with the message of the poem is not mentioned either. C) He didn't understand the meaning of the poem is not indicated in the passage. Lastly, the passage does not provide any information about finding the poem boring or lacking comprehension. Hence, the correct answer is D) He repeated the lines of the poem based on the given information in the passage.

16. A) A jadestone pendant.

Explanation: According to the passage, Mr. Spring Fragrance found a little box in his pocket. Inside the box was a jadestone pendant that he had bought for Mrs. Spring Fragrance as a gift on their fifth wedding anniversary. Therefore, the correct answer is A) A jadestone pendant.

The other choices are incorrect because they are not mentioned in the passage. B) A poem written by Tennyson is not mentioned as being found in Mr. Spring Fragrance's pocket. C) A box of chocolates is not mentioned in the passage. D) Laura's love letter is also not mentioned in the given text. Hence, the correct answer is A) A jadestone pendant based on the information provided.

17. C) -ly.

Explanation: The suffix in the word "suddenly" is "-ly." The suffix "-ly" is commonly used to form adverbs from adjectives, indicating the manner in which an action is performed. In this case, the adverb "suddenly" is formed from the adjective "sudden." Therefore, the correct answer is C) -ly.

The other choices are incorrect because they do not accurately represent the suffix in the word "suddenly." A) -enly, B) -nly, and D) -y are not valid suffixes for this word. Hence, the correct answer is C) -ly based on the rules of word formation and the given word.

The Dragon Tamers - E. Nesbit

18. C) In a ruinous castle

John the blacksmith set up his forge in a ruinous castle (C). The passage mentions that the castle was old and in ruins, and only two little rooms remained. Since John was too poor to live in a proper house, he found a place in the castle where he could work. This choice is supported by the sentence "So there John blew his bellows and hammered his iron and did all the work which came his way." It is clear that he was working in the castle, not in a proper house or in the mayor's large forge. The passage also states that the mayor of the town had a large forge facing the town square, where most of the trade went, which eliminates the option of John setting up his forge in the town square (D). The option of setting up his forge in the mayor's large forge (B) is also incorrect because the passage clearly mentions that the mayor had his own forge with apprentices and journeymen working for him. Therefore, the correct choice is C, a ruinous castle, as it is the only option consistent with the details provided in the passage.

Grade 5 — Ans keys

19. D) Because it was the only available storage space

John the blacksmith kept his old iron and other materials in the dungeon because it was the only available storage space (D). The passage mentions that the two rooms in the ruinous castle where John lived and worked were not very large. Therefore, he needed additional space to store his items, and the dungeon was the only option mentioned in the text. The options A and B, warm and weather-tight, and a vaulted roof, respectively, are characteristics of the dungeon, but they are not the reasons specifically mentioned for why John chose to store his materials there. The option C, convenient for tying captives, is mentioned as a feature of the dungeon, but it is not stated that John used it for that purpose. Therefore, the correct choice is D, because it was the only available storage space, as this is the reason directly supported by the passage.

20. C) Sent them down the broken flight of steps

The lords of the castle sent prisoners down the broken flight of steps (C). The passage mentions that the lords of the castle would kick prisoners down the steps in a lighthearted and hopeful way, and the prisoners never came back. This implies that the prisoners were sent down the steps as a form of punishment or disposal, and it suggests that it was a permanent action. The option A, sending prisoners to work in the blacksmith's forge, is not mentioned in the passage and does not align with the context provided. The option B, releasing prisoners after a short time, is contradicted by the statement that the prisoners never came back. The option D, giving them a fair trial and punishment, is not supported by the passage, which implies a more arbitrary and cruel treatment of prisoners. Therefore, the correct choice is C, sending them down the broken flight of steps, as it is the action described in the passage.

21. C) Because she was tired from taking care of the baby

John the blacksmith's wife cried because she was tired from taking care of the baby (C). The passage mentions that the baby cried at night, which prevented the mother from getting enough rest. It states, "This made her very tired." This indicates that the mother was exhausted from the baby's crying and the resulting lack of sleep. The option A, missing her father's cows, is not mentioned in the passage and does not relate to the reason for her crying. The option B, John's hair getting gray, is mentioned as a detail about John's appearance but not directly connected to the wife's crying. The option D, not having enough to eat, is mentioned in relation to John's financial struggles but is not specifically mentioned as a reason for the wife's tears. Therefore, the correct choice is C, because she was tired from taking care of the baby, as it is the reason directly supported by the passage.

22. B) The mayor's forge has a self-acting hammer and electric bellows.

In the passage, it is mentioned that the mayor of the town, who is also a blacksmith, has a large forge facing the town square. The text describes the mayor's forge as having "a patent forge and a self-acting hammer and electric bellows." These advanced tools and equipment indicate that the mayor's forge is more technologically advanced and sophisticated compared to John the blacksmith's forge.

Option A, the mayor's forge being located in a proper house, is not mentioned in the text. Option C, the mayor's forge being situated in the countryside, is not supported by the passage, which states that the mayor's forge is located in the town square. Option D, the mayor's forge being operated by twelve apprentices, is also not mentioned in the passage. Therefore, the best answer is B) The mayor's forge has a self-acting hammer and electric bellows, as it is explicitly stated in the text.

23. **C) 3 - the remains of a building, city, etc.**

The passage describes an old, old castle where the walls, towers, turrets, gateways, and arches have crumbled to ruins. It specifically mentions that "of all its old splendor there were only two little rooms left." This indicates that the castle has deteriorated, and only two small rooms are remaining, which aligns with the definition of ruins as the remains of a building.

Option A) 1 refers to reducing something to a fallen or decayed condition, which is not the case in the passage. Option B) 2 pertains to bringing a person or company to financial destruction, which is not directly mentioned in the passage. Option D) 4 refers to coming to downfall or destruction, which is a more general sense and does not specifically address the condition of the castle.

24. **D) Because the mayor had a large forge with advanced equipment.**

In the passage, it is mentioned that the mayor of the town operated a large forge facing the town square. The text describes the mayor's forge as having a "huge forge" with advanced features such as a "patent forge," a "self-acting hammer," and "electric bellows." These details indicate that the mayor's forge was equipped with modern and efficient tools, making it more capable of handling a larger volume of work.

Option A) Because the townspeople did not know about John's forge is not supported by the passage. Option B) Because the mayor's apprentices were more skilled is not mentioned in the passage. Option C) Because the mayor had lower prices than John the blacksmith is not specifically mentioned as a reason in the passage.

25. **B) His odds and ends and coal.**

According to the passage, John the blacksmith kept his "old iron, his odds and ends, his fagots, and his two pence worth of coal" in the great dungeon under the castle. This indicates that the items he stored in the dungeon were miscellaneous materials such as scraps, leftover pieces, and small quantities of coal used for fuel in his forge.

Option A) His family's belongings is not mentioned in the passage as being stored in the dungeon. Option C) His tools and equipment are not specified as being stored in the dungeon, although it can be assumed that he kept them in his forge. Option D) His customers' orders is not mentioned as being stored in the dungeon; it refers to the work that John undertakes rather than items stored in the dungeon.

26. **B) A dilapidated castle with ruins and two small rooms.**

According to the description in the passage, the castle is described as "old" and in a state of ruin, with its walls, towers, turrets, gateways, and arches crumbled to ruins. The passage further mentions that only "two little rooms" are left in the castle. Therefore, the accurate description would be a phrase describing a dilapidated castle with ruins and two small rooms.

Option A) A grand castle with intact walls and towers does not match the description of the ruinous castle in the passage. Option C) bustling town square with a large forge does not represent the specific location where John the blacksmith set up his forge within the castle ruins. Option D) A modern blacksmith's workshop with advanced equipment is not aligned with the setting of the story, which takes place in a dilapidated castle with limited resources.

THE YOUNG KING – OSCAR WILDE

27. A) The Great Hall of the Palace

Explanation: After taking their leave of the young King, the courtiers went to the Great Hall of the Palace. The passage mentions that they retired there to receive a few last lessons from the Professor of Etiquette. The courtiers needed to learn and adhere to the proper manners and customs expected of them in the court, as natural manners were considered a grave offense for a courtier. Therefore, they went to the Great Hall to receive these lessons and prepare themselves for the upcoming coronation.

The other choices (B) The Chamber of Secrets, (C) The Royal Gardens, and (D) The Professor's Quarters are incorrect. The passage does not mention anything about a Chamber of Secrets or Royal Gardens in relation to where the courtiers went after leaving the young King. The mention of the Professor of Etiquette implies that they were going to a place where etiquette lessons would be held, rather than the Professor's private quarters. Thus, the correct choice is (A) The Great Hall of the Palace.

28. A) Relieved

Explanation: The passage states that when the courtiers took their leave of the young King, he flung himself back on his couch with a deep sigh of relief. This indicates that he felt relieved when they left. The passage further describes him as wild-eyed and open-mouthed, appearing like a young animal or a woodland faun that had been newly snared by hunters. This imagery suggests a sense of freedom and relief from the formalities and expectations that surrounded him in the presence of the courtiers. Therefore, the correct choice is (A) Relieved.

The other choices (B) Disappointed, (C) Angry, and (D) Indifferent are incorrect. The passage does not provide any indication or description that the young King felt disappointed, angry, or indifferent when the courtiers left. Instead, it explicitly states that he sighed with relief, which suggests a positive emotional response to their departure.

29. C) Both A) and B)

Explanation: The passage presents two possible reasons for the death of the young King's mother. It mentions that the court physician stated that it was either grief or the plague that caused her death.

Additionally, it suggests that some people speculated that she might have been killed by a swift Italian poison administered in a cup of spiced wine. The passage does not explicitly state which of these reasons is true, but it presents both possibilities. Therefore, the correct choice is (C) Both A) and B), as the passage mentions both grief or the plague as well as the suggestion of a swift Italian poison.

The other choice, (D) The text does not provide a clear reason, is incorrect. While the passage does not definitively state the exact cause of the young King's mother's death, it does provide two possible explanations, indicating that the reason is not completely unknown or unclear.

30. **D) All of the above.**

Explanation: All of the provided options suggest a mysterious and potentially sinister backstory regarding the young King's mother's burial. A) The fact that she was buried in a deserted churchyard adds an eerie and mysterious element to her burial. The use of the term "deserted" implies neglect or abandonment, raising questions about why such a location was chosen for her final resting place. B) The mention of another body, that of a young man with stab wounds, being buried alongside her intensifies the sense of intrigue and potential foul play. The presence of a deceased young man with apparent signs of violence suggests a connection between the two deaths and raises suspicions about the circumstances surrounding their deaths. C) The description of the grave being dug beyond the city gates further contributes to the mysterious atmosphere. Burial beyond the city gates implies a separation from the regular burial grounds and signifies a hidden or secretive act.

31. **A) Tapped lightly**

Explanation: The word 'knocked' in this sentence means to tap lightly. When someone knocks at a door, they gently strike or tap on it to get attention. The other choices are incorrect because 'banged forcefully' suggests a loud and strong impact, which is not indicated in the sentence. 'Scratched gently' implies using nails or fingers to create a light abrasion, which is not relevant to the context of knocking on a door. 'Pushed open' means to apply force and open the door, which is not what the word 'knocked' signifies. Therefore, the correct answer is (A) Tapped lightly, as it best aligns with the action described in the sentence.

'Banged forcefully' (choice B) suggests a strong and loud impact, which does not align with the gentle action of knocking on a door. The sentence does not provide any indication of forceful banging. 'Scratched gently' (choice C) implies a light scratching motion, which is not relevant to the act of knocking on a door. Knocking involves creating a sound by striking or tapping on a door, not by scratching it. 'Pushed open' (choice D) refers to physically applying force to open a door, which is different from the action of knocking. The sentence specifically mentions knocking at the door, not pushing it open.

32. **B) 2**

Explanation: In paragraph 1, the word 'grave' is used to describe the courtiers' manners as "serious and solemn in manner or appearance." The passage mentions that the courtiers bowed their heads to the ground, according to the ceremonious usage of the day. This suggests a formal and respectful behavior, indicating seriousness and solemnity. Therefore, the correct choice is (B) 2, as it aligns with the context of the courtiers' behavior.

The other choices (A) 1, (C) 3, and (D) 4 are incorrect. The passage does not refer to a literal hole dug in the ground for burying a dead body, which is the meaning provided in choice (A) 1. The context does not involve any pressure, rubbing, or marks, ruling out choice (C) 3. Additionally, the passage does not mention any slow and solemn musical composition, which is the meaning provided in choice (D) 4. Therefore, the correct choice is (B) 2, indicating a serious and solemn manner.

33. **D) The text does not specify their exact relationship.**

Explanation: The passage does not provide clear information about the exact relationship between the young King and the old King. It mentions that the young King is the child of the old King's only daughter, who had a secret marriage with someone of lower status. However, the passage does not explicitly state whether the old King is the young King's father, uncle, or grandfather. The lack of specific details about their familial connection indicates that the text does not provide a clear answer regarding their relationship. Therefore, the correct choice is (D) The text does not specify their exact relationship.

The other choices, (A) He is the old King's son, (B) He is the old King's nephew, and (C) He is the old King's grandson, are all incorrect because the passage does not provide evidence to support any of these specific relationships. While it mentions that the young King is the child of the old King's daughter, it does not reveal the exact paternal or maternal connection to the old King. Therefore, none of these options can be confirmed based on the information given in the passage.

34. **C) In the presence of the Council**

Explanation: According to the passage, the old King acknowledged the young King as his heir in the presence of the Council. The text mentions that when the old King was on his deathbed, he had the lad sent for and made the acknowledgment in front of the Council. This suggests that the decision was made public and involved the presence and approval of the Council members. Therefore, the correct choice is (C) In the presence of the Council.

The other choices are incorrect because the passage does not mention them as the specific means through which the old King acknowledged the young King as his heir. The text does not refer to a public proclamation (choice A) or a private letter (choice B) as the methods used. Additionally, it is not stated in the passage that the method of acknowledgment is not mentioned (choice D). Therefore, based on the information provided, the correct choice is (C) In the presence of the Council.

35. **B) The old King's remorse for a past sin**

Explanation: The passage suggests that the old King's decision to make the young King his heir was prompted by his remorse for a past sin. It states that the old King, when on his deathbed, was moved by remorse for his great sin or wrongdoing. This suggests that the old King felt guilt or regret for something he had done in the past, leading him to choose the young King as his heir. The passage does not mention the young King's exceptional musical talent (choice A) or his popularity among the people (choice C) as factors influencing the old King's decision. Nor does it mention the Council's recommendation (choice D) as the basis for the decision. Therefore, based on the information provided, the correct choice is (B) The old King's remorse for a past sin.

36. **D) The Boys Who Stopped the Band: A Tale of Bravery in Nottinghamshire.**

This title accurately captures the main focus of the story, which revolves around the heroic actions of the two boys, William, and Thomas, in defeating the band of robbers. It emphasizes their courage and bravery, highlighting their role in bringing justice to their community. The title also mentions the specific setting, Nottinghamshire, providing context and adding to the excitement of the tale.

The other choices are incorrect because they either do not convey the central theme of the story or lack specificity. Option A, "Shadows of Justice: The Heroic Journey of William and Thomas," focuses more on justice and the boys' journey rather than their specific accomplishment of stopping the band of robbers. Option B, "Robbers' Defeat: The Unlikely Triumph of Two Young Boys," emphasizes the defeat of the robbers but does not highlight the bravery and heroism of William and Thomas. Option C, "Adventures in Nottinghamshire: The Courageous Exploits of William and Thomas," is too broad and does not specifically mention the boys' achievement of stopping the band of robbers. Therefore, based on the story's content, the most suitable title is D) The Boys Who Stopped the Band: A Tale of Bravery in Nottinghamshire.

37. **C) Heroic accomplishments.**

This phrase captures the idea that the actions of William and Thomas were not only admirable and courageous but also had a heroic impact. It highlights the significance and impact of their actions in standing up against injustice and stopping the band of robbers.

The other choices, while related in meaning, do not fully encompass the depth and impact of the boys' actions. Option A, "courageous acts," focuses more on bravery but may not fully convey the sense of significance and impact. Option B, "admirable actions," suggests that their deeds are praiseworthy but does not emphasize the heroic nature of their accomplishments. Option D, "valiant endeavors," captures the bravery and determination but does not specifically highlight the noble and heroic aspects of their actions. Therefore, based on the context and the impact of their actions, C) Heroic accomplishments is the most suitable synonym for "noble deeds."

38. **A) To tell us about the time and place of the story.**

The paragraph provides information about the setting, which is Nottinghamshire, England, in the early 19th century. It tells us that the story takes place a long time ago in a specific town. The paragraph mentions economic hardship and the band of robbers, but it doesn't explain the problems faced by the town in detail, so choice B is incorrect. While the paragraph briefly introduces the characters William and Thomas, it doesn't focus on their friendship, so choice D is incorrect. The primary purpose of the paragraph is to establish the time and place, giving the readers a sense of where and when the story unfolds.

Paragraph 1 begins with "Once upon a time, in the early 19th century, in the picturesque town of Nottinghamshire, England," which immediately tells us about the time and place of the story. It sets the historical context by mentioning the early 19th century and the specific location of Nottinghamshire, England. The paragraph goes on to mention economic hardship and the notorious band of robbers, but it doesn't go into detail about the problems faced by the town, so choice B is incorrect. While the paragraph introduces the characters William and Thomas, it does not delve into their friendship or focus on it as the main reason for the paragraph, so choice D is incorrect. The primary purpose of the paragraph is to provide the time and place of the story, giving the readers a sense of where and when the events take place. Therefore, choice A is the correct answer.

39. **A) Sherwood Forest.**

In paragraph 3, it is mentioned that as the boys ventured into Sherwood Forest to explore, they stumbled upon a hidden cave. This indicates that Sherwood Forest is the location where they discovered the cave. Choices B, C, and D are incorrect because the passage does not mention the cave being located in the Nottinghamshire village, William's farm, or Constable Albert's house.

40. **B) The villagers**

According to the passage, B) The villagers assisted William and Thomas in their mission to stop the robbers. In paragraph 7, it is mentioned that under the cover of darkness, the trio infiltrated the cave with the assistance of a small group of trusted villagers. This indicates that the villagers supported them in their endeavor to apprehend the robbers. Choices A, C, and D are incorrect because the passage does not mention the local authorities, the robbers' gang, or Constable Albert's family assisting them in their mission.

41. **C) They hailed them as heroes**

According to the passage, C) The townsfolk hailed William and Thomas as heroes. In paragraph 10, it is mentioned that news of their bravery spread quickly throughout Nottinghamshire, and the townsfolk celebrated them for their ingenuity, resilience, and selflessness. They were presented with commendations by the local authorities, and their families were proud of them. This indicates that the townsfolk had a positive and appreciative reaction to their actions. Choices A, B, and D are incorrect because the passage does not mention criticism, ignorance, or doubt from the townsfolk regarding William and Thomas's bravery.

42. **A) The arrangement or organization of objects, elements, or information in a particular space or design.**

In this sentence, it refers to the way the cave is structured or arranged, including its various features, rooms, and passages. The boys observed the robbers' activities and learned not only their routines but also how the cave was set up, allowing them to navigate it effectively during their mission.

Choices B, C, and D are incorrect. Choice B refers to a plot of land for agricultural purposes, which is unrelated to the meaning in the passage. Choice C refers to the process of drawing or designing the outline or structure of something, which is not the intended meaning in this context. Choice D refers to a plan or blueprint for the construction of a building or infrastructure, which is also not the intended meaning in the passage.

Preserving the Jewels of the Sea: Combating the Depletion of Coral Reefs

43. B) Rising sea temperatures and coral bleaching.

The passage explains that as a result of global warming, rising sea temperatures cause coral bleaching, where corals expel the symbiotic algae within their tissues, leading to their vulnerability to disease and turning them white. The increased frequency and severity of coral bleaching events have resulted in once vibrant reefs becoming devoid of life.

Choices A, C, and D are incorrect. Choice A, overfishing and destructive fishing practices, is mentioned in paragraph 3 as another factor contributing to coral reef depletion. Choice C, pollution from land-based sources, is discussed in paragraph 4 as another significant threat to coral reefs. Choice D, storms and hurricanes, is mentioned in paragraph 5 as a natural phenomenon that impacts coral reefs but is not identified as a significant factor contributing to their depletion.

44. C) Imbalances in population.

In paragraph 3, it is mentioned that unsustainable fishing practices, such as blast fishing and the use of cyanide, not only harm coral colonies directly but also disrupt the delicate balance of the reef ecosystem. By removing key fish species from the food chain through overfishing, imbalances in population can occur, which negatively affects the overall health and stability of the coral reef ecosystem.

Choices A, B, and D are incorrect. Coral bleaching is discussed in paragraph 2 as a consequence of rising sea temperatures, not unsustainable fishing practices. Coastal protection from storms is mentioned in paragraph 6 as one of the essential ecosystem services provided by coral reefs but is not directly related to unsustainable fishing practices. Sediment and chemical pollutants are discussed in paragraph 4 as a result of pollution from land-based sources, not unsustainable fishing practices.

45. C) Runoff from agricultural activities and sewage discharge.

In paragraph 4, it is mentioned that pollution from land-based sources poses a significant threat to coral reefs. Examples of land-based sources of pollution include runoff from agricultural activities, which can introduce high levels of sediment, nutrients, and chemical pollutants into coastal waters. Sewage discharge, which involves the release of untreated or inadequately treated wastewater into marine environments, is another land-based source of pollution that can negatively impact coral reefs.

Choices A, B, and D are incorrect. Rising sea temperatures and coral bleaching are discussed in paragraph 2 as a factor contributing to the depletion of coral reefs, but they are not land-based sources of pollution. Violent storms and hurricanes are mentioned in paragraph 5 as natural phenomena that can physically damage coral structures, but they are not land-based sources of pollution. Coral nurseries and artificial reef structures are mentioned in paragraph 7 as coral restoration projects, but they are not examples of land-based sources of pollution.

Grade 5 — Ans keys

46. A) Coastal protection from storms and shoreline stabilization.

In paragraph 6, it is stated that coral reefs provide essential ecosystem services, which include coastal protection from storms and shoreline stabilization. Coral reefs act as natural barriers that reduce the impact of waves and storms, helping to protect coastal areas from erosion and flooding.

Choices B, C, and D are incorrect. Rising sea temperatures and coral bleaching, mentioned in choice B, are factors contributing to the depletion of coral reefs discussed in paragraph 2, but they are not ecosystem services provided by coral reefs. Sustainable fishing practices and water quality improvement, mentioned in choice C, are conservation initiatives and actions taken to reduce the depletion of coral reefs, but they are not ecosystem services provided by coral reefs themselves. Choice D mentions tourism, recreational activities, and fishing

industries, which are economic benefits associated with coral reefs, but they are not ecosystem services provided by coral reefs.

47. A) Reducing greenhouse gas emissions and improving water quality.

In paragraph 7, it is mentioned that conservation initiatives focus on reducing greenhouse gas emissions to combat climate change, implementing sustainable fishing practices, and improving water quality through better management of coastal activities. These initiatives are aimed at addressing the root causes of reef depletion and promoting the conservation and restoration of coral reefs.

Choice B, overfishing and destructive fishing practices, is mentioned as a factor contributing to the depletion of coral reefs in paragraph 3, but it is not mentioned as a conservation initiative to reduce depletion. Choices C and D, violent storms and hurricanes, and coral bleaching and ocean acidification, are mentioned as natural phenomena and factors impacting coral reefs, but they are not conservation initiatives.

48. C) Efforts to protect and restore coral reefs are crucial.

In the concluding paragraph (paragraph 8), it is stated that the depletion of coral reefs is an urgent issue and emphasizes the importance of recognizing the value of these ecosystems and taking action to protect and restore them. The paragraph emphasizes the need to address the root causes of reef depletion and implement sustainable practices to ensure the preservation of coral reefs for future generations.

While choices A, B, and D mention various aspects related to coral reefs, such as their vibrant ecosystems, the factors depleting them (rising sea temperatures and overfishing), and the ecosystem services they provide, they do not capture the main message conveyed in the concluding paragraph, which is the importance of conservation and restoration efforts.

49. C) Bleached and white coral colonies.

When corals are stressed, they expel the algae living within them, causing them to turn white or bleach. This is a sign of poor health and can indicate a depleted coral reef. Healthy coral colonies are usually colorful and vibrant, so the presence of bleached and white coral colonies suggests a decline in the health of the reef ecosystem. Option A is incorrect because colorful and healthy coral colonies are a sign of a healthy reef.

Option B is incorrect because a school of vibrant fish swimming around the corals can be present in both healthy and depleted reef environments. Option D is incorrect because various sizes and shapes of coral structures do not necessarily indicate the health of the reef. It is the condition of the coral colonies themselves, specifically the bleached and white appearance, that points to a depleted reef.

50. **B) A place where young plants and trees are grown and nurtured.**

In the context of the passage, the term "coral nurseries" refers to specific areas or structures where fragments of coral are cultivated and allowed to grow and develop. These nurseries serve as a means to restore damaged or depleted coral reefs by providing a controlled environment for the growth and propagation of corals. The purpose is similar to that of a plant nursery, where young plants are nurtured and cared for until they are ready to be transplanted into their natural habitat. Option A is incorrect because it refers to a different kind of nursery involving the care of young children. Option C is incorrect because it pertains to a medical facility specializing in newborn care. Option D is incorrect because it relates to a school or institution for the education of young children.

Grade 5

Ans keys

JO'S JOURNAL

1. **A. New York**

Explanation: The narrator is writing from New York, as indicated in the text when she mentions her journey and arrival at Mrs. Kirke's house in New York. She describes her experiences and interactions with Mrs. Kirke, the children, and Professor Bhaer, who is from Berlin. The narrator also mentions seeing Professor Bhaer carrying a hod of coal and refers to him as someone who helps others. The other choices (B. Berlin, C. Ireland, D. Chicago) are incorrect because the text clearly states that the narrator is in New York, where she has taken up a position as a governess and is settling into her new surroundings.

2. **B. The parlour and the nursery**

Explanation: The glass door separates the parlour and the nursery. In the passage, the narrator mentions that there is a glass door between Mrs. Kirke's parlour and the nursery where she is to teach and sew. This glass door allows her to observe Professor Bhaer, who uses the parlour for his lessons, and she expresses her intention to peep at him and describe his appearance in the future. The other choices (A. The living room and the dining room, C. The study and the bedroom, D. The parlour and the kitchen) are incorrect because the text does not mention any such separations or interactions between those rooms.

3. **A. To support himself and his orphan nephews**

Explanation: In the passage, it is mentioned that Professor Bhaer gives lessons to support himself and his two little orphan nephews. He is described as poor but learned, and he takes on teaching to provide for his own livelihood and to educate his nephews, as per his sister's wishes. The other choices (B. To learn new things, C. To earn his living as he was as poor as a door-mouse, D. To teach his orphan nephews) do not accurately reflect the reason given in the passage for Professor Bhaer's decision to give lessons.

4. **D. 4**

Explanation: The word "atone" has meanings related to making up for a wrong or reconciling (options 1, 2, and 3), but it does not mean "along with" (option 4). The other choices reflect accurate meanings of the word as per the context.

5. **D. The children were pampered, and it wasn't until she told them The Seven Bad Pigs that they cherished her.**

Explanation: The statement in option d is not true based on the passage. Jo mentions that the children took to her after she told them The Seven Bad Pigs, indicating that they appreciated her after this incident, which suggests that they were not initially pampered or cherished her before that. The other options accurately describe Jo's stay at the house as mentioned in the passage.

Grade 5

Ans keys

6. **A. I, II, III**

Explanation: Mrs. K, welcomed Jo and encouraged her to make herself at home in several ways. Firstly, she assured Jo that her rooms were always open for her, creating a sense of warmth and hospitality. Secondly, Mrs. K took care to make Jo's room as comfortable as possible, ensuring that she had a cozy and pleasant space. Thirdly, Mrs. K offered to make Jo a cup of tea whenever she wanted to talk, indicating her willingness to engage and provide a friendly environment. These actions collectively demonstrate Mrs. K's effort to make Jo feel comfortable and welcome in her new surroundings. Option B is incorrect because it includes "IV. If she wanted to socialize, there were a lot of pleasant people in the house," which is not mentioned in the passage as a specific action taken by Mrs. K to make Jo feel at home. Option C is incorrect because it does not include the correct combination of statements, and option D is incorrect because it includes "III" which is not mentioned in the passage.

7. **D. something of little value, substance, or importance**

Explanation: In the context of the phrase "trifles show character," the word "trifles" refers to things that are of little value or importance. The phrase suggests that small or seemingly insignificant actions or details can reveal or reflect a person's true character. The idea is that paying attention to small or trivial matters can provide insights into someone's personality or qualities. Options A, B, and C do not fit the context of the phrase in the given passage.

8. **C. Journal letter**

Explanation: The text is written in the form of a journal letter. The narrator addresses the letter to "Marmee and Beth," which suggests personal and informal communication. The narrator shares personal experiences, thoughts, and details of their stay, similar to a journal entry. The content and tone of the text resemble a letter written in a journal-style format. Options A, B, and D do not accurately describe the form of the text as well as option C does.

"MY HOUSE IS HAUNTED" - Heidi
By Johanna Spyri

9. **C. She believed someone might be following her.**

Explanation: Miss Rottermeyer called Tinette to accompany her in certain areas of the house because she believed someone might be following her or coming up behind her silently. The passage describes how Miss Rottermeyer looked cautiously behind her and into dark corners as if she thought someone might unexpectedly give her dress a pull. This suggests her fear of being followed or pursued. Option A (needing help carrying something) and option B (afraid of the dark) do not accurately capture the context of the passage, as it focuses on Miss Rottermeyer's sense of being followed. Option D (wanting a companion for conversation) also does not reflect the specific reason mentioned in the passage.

Grade 5

Ans keys

10. **D. The front door wide open**

Explanation: The servants found the front door wide open every morning when they went downstairs. The passage mentions that the front door was found open despite there being nobody far or near to account for it. This mysterious occurrence puzzled the household, leading them to search for a possible explanation. Options A (broken windows) and B (missing items from the house) are not mentioned as outcomes of this strange event. Option C (a thief hiding in the house) is considered as a possibility initially, but it is later revealed that nothing in the house had been touched, ruling out the presence of a thief.

11. **B. A thief had been hiding in the house and stolen goods**

Explanation: The general idea among the household members was that a thief had been hiding in the house and had gone off in the night with stolen goods. This is mentioned in the passage as the initial assumption when the front door was found wide open every morning. The servants were alarmed and searched every room and corner to check if anything had been stolen. Option A (servants forgot to lock it properly) is not mentioned in the passage as a reason. Option C (the door was malfunctioning) is also not mentioned as a possibility. Option D (the wind had blown it open) is not considered as the cause of the door being open, as the passage later describes a sudden gust of air blowing through the door and putting out a light, suggesting something more mysterious than just wind.

12. **A. Drank brandy and gathered weapons**

Explanation: Sebastian and John prepared for their night of watching by drinking brandy (strengthening cordial) to boost their courage and gathering weapons belonging to the master, as well as a bottle of brandy. This is mentioned in the passage when Miss Rottermeyer gave them the brandy and weapons so that their courage would not fail if they had to confront anything unusual during the night. The other options (B, C, and D) are not mentioned in the passage as preparations made by Sebastian and John.

13. **D. John was trembling all over and as white as a ghost**

Explanation: Sebastian gave a cry of alarm when he saw John in the light because John was trembling all over and as white as a ghost. This is mentioned in the passage after John had opened the front door and then quickly shut it again after a sudden gust of air blew out the light he was holding. John's frightened and pale appearance alarmed Sebastian, leading him to exclaim in alarm. The other options (A, B, and C) are not accurate descriptions of the reason for Sebastian's cry of alarm.

14. **A. Because she was experiencing health issues**

Explanation: Clara initially insisted that her father come home because she was experiencing health issues. In the passage, it is mentioned that Miss Rottermeyer wrote to Mr. Sesemann, stating that the unaccountable things going on in the house had affected Clara's delicate constitution and that the worst consequences might be expected, including the possibility of epileptic fits and St. Vitus's dance. This health concern prompted Clara to want her father to return home to address her well-being. The other options (B, C, and D) are not explicitly supported by the passage as the primary reason for Clara's insistence.

15. B. He arranged to come home two days later.

Explanation: In the passage, it is mentioned that Mr. Sesemann arranged to come home two days later upon receiving the second letter about the unaccountable things happening in the house and their impact on Clara's health. The other options are incorrect because they do not align with the information provided in the passage.

16. B. the physical makeup of the individual, especially with respect to the health, strength, and appearance of the body.

Explanation: In this context, the word "constitution" refers to the physical health and well-being of Clara. The sentence indicates that the unexplained events in the house have negatively affected Clara's delicate physical condition, potentially leading to adverse health consequences. The other options do not accurately capture the intended meaning in this context.

THE FIRST VOYAGE OF SINDBAD THE SAILOR

17. C. walk in his father's ways.

Explanation: After his father's death, Sindbad resolved to follow in his father's footsteps and lead a life similar to his father's honorable and wise ways. He wanted to learn from his father's teachings and wisdom, especially valuing the importance of a good reputation and proper use of his inheritance. The other options do not accurately capture Sindbad's decision and intention mentioned in the passage.

18. B. an island in the Indies.

Explanation: After setting sail towards the Indies, Sindbad and the other merchants disembarked from their ship for the first time on an island that appeared to be a green meadow rising slightly above the water. This island was one of the islands they encountered during their voyage, and it is described in the passage. The other options do not accurately describe the location where they disembarked.

19. C. the island trembled and shook.

Explanation: While Sindbad and the merchants were on the small island, they experienced a sudden and unexpected event—the island started to tremble and shake. This event was a result of the island being the back of a sea monster, as revealed later in the passage. The other options do not accurately describe the event that occurred while they were on the island.

Grade 5

Ans keys

20. **A. grooms belonging to the sovereign.**

Explanation: Sindbad met grooms belonging to the sovereign of the island in the cave. These grooms were responsible for taking care of the king's horses and bringing them to the island for pasturage. They were about to return home, and their presence and assistance were crucial for Sindbad's survival and rescue. The other options do not accurately describe the individuals Sindbad encountered in the cave.

21. **A. A good reputation is better than expensive ointment which wears off with time.**

Explanation: The phrase "a good name is better than precious ointment" means that having a good reputation and being respected by others is more valuable and enduring than material possessions or external beauty. Just as ointment might lose its fragrance and value over time, material things can diminish in importance, but a person's good name and reputation have lasting worth. This saying emphasizes the importance of cultivating a positive character and being held in high esteem by others. The other options do not accurately capture the meaning of the phrase.

22. **B. The Great Pyramid inclines at an angle of about 51.5 degrees to the top.**

Explanation: This choice accurately reflects the usage of the word "inclined" in the passage, describing the angle at which the pyramid is slanted. The other options do not match the specific context of the paragraph: option A talks about a person's head position, option C refers to a physical slope, and option D relates to a personal tendency, none of which align with the description of the pyramid's slant.

23. **A. a fore-and-aft rigged boat with one mast and a single jib.**

Explanation: In the context of the passage, a sloop refers to a specific type of sailing vessel with a single mast and a jib sail that is set forward of the mast. The other options do not match the meaning of a sloop in this context: option B refers to the diameter of an optical system, option C refers to an animal's burrow, and option D describes the act of hiding in such a burrow.

24. **C. The captain believed that Sinbad was dead, and therefore he thought that the man was an imposter.**

Explanation: In this paragraph, the captain initially doubts Sindbad's identity because he

had believed that Sindbad had perished. The captain's skepticism arises from thinking that Sindbad, who was presumed dead, could not possibly be alive. This doubt is based on the mistaken assumption that Sindbad had met his end. The other options do not accurately capture the main idea of this paragraph: option A is not the primary focus, and options B

and D do not reflect the captain's suspicion regarding Sindbad's identity.

25. **B. Ginger ale.**

Explanation: In the passage, it is mentioned that Sindbad brought back "wood of aloes, sandals, camphire, nutmegs, cloves, pepper, and ginger." While ginger is mentioned, there is no mention of ginger ale. The other items listed in options A, C, and D are all mentioned as being brought back by Sindbad.

THE ADVENTURES OF TOM SAWYER

By Mark Twain

26. **D. To find Tom.**

Explanation: The old lady put her spectacles on to look for Tom. In the passage, it's mentioned that she pulled her spectacles down and looked over the room, then put them up and looked out under them. She used her spectacles to search for Tom, wondering where he was. The other choices are incorrect because option a mentions looking around the room, which is only part of what she did, and options b and c are not mentioned in the passage as reasons for her putting on her spectacles.

27. **B. The closet.**

Explanation: The old lady goes to the closet to look for Tom. In the passage, it's mentioned that she turned and seized a small boy by the slack of his roundabout and arrested his flight. She then asks him what he has been doing in the closet. The other choices are incorrect because none of them accurately describe where the old lady goes to look for Tom.

28. **C. Tricking her and then distracting her.**

Explanation: In this sentence, 'that' refers to the tricks that Tom has played on her in the past, which involve tricking her and then distracting her. The old lady is expressing frustration that Tom has played enough tricks like this for her to have learned to be more cautious and watchful of his actions. The other choices do not accurately capture the meaning of 'that' in the context of the sentence.

29. **D. If you don't discipline a child, they will become spoiled.**

Explanation: The phrase "spare the rod and spile the child" means that if you avoid disciplining or punishing a child (by not using the rod, which symbolizes physical discipline), the child will become spoiled and unruly. Aunt Polly expresses the idea that proper discipline is necessary to prevent a child from becoming spoiled or misbehaved. The other choices do not accurately capture the meaning of the phrase in the context of the sentence.

30. **D. To do her duty by him as his guardian.**

Explanation: Aunt Polly mentions that she'll make Tom work on Saturdays to do her duty by him as his guardian. She acknowledges that she needs to discipline him and ensure he learns responsibility, even if he dislikes work on weekends when other boys are having a holiday. The other choices may be related to Tom working, but they don't directly capture the reason Aunt Polly gives for making him work on Saturdays.

31. **B. Her conscience hurts.**

Explanation: Aunt Polly mentions that every time she lets Tom off without punishment, her conscience hurts. She knows that she's not fulfilling her duty as his guardian and that she's allowing him to get away with his mischievous behavior. The other choices do not accurately reflect her feelings of guilt and responsibility for not disciplining Tom.

Grade 5 — Ans keys

32. B. Succeed in.

Explanation: In this context, "make out" means to succeed in or manage to achieve. Aunt Polly is expressing how Tom seems to know exactly how to manipulate her emotions and behaviors to avoid punishment. The phrase "make out to put me off for a minute or make me laugh" indicates that Tom is skilled at diverting her attention or making her laugh to avoid getting into trouble. The other options do not fit the context in which the phrase is used.

33. D. Of few days and full of trouble.

Explanation: According to Aunt Polly, the phrase "man that is born of woman is of few days and full of trouble" reflects her belief that human life is short and filled with challenges and difficulties. This phrase suggests that life is inherently challenging, and that people experience various troubles and hardships throughout their lives. The other options do not capture the sense of challenges and difficulties that Aunt Polly is conveying in her statement.

34. A. Be the ruination of the child.

Explanation: Aunt Polly fears that if she doesn't discipline Tom, she will be the cause of his downfall or ruin. She believes that sparing the rod and not properly disciplining him will lead to negative consequences for Tom's character and behavior. The phrase "Spare the rod and spile the child" implies that without proper discipline, a child's behavior and development could be negatively affected. The other options do not capture Aunt Polly's specific concern about the long-term impact of not disciplining Tom.

JANE GOODALL

35. D. By immersing herself in their habitat.

Explanation: Jane Goodall took an unorthodox approach to her research on chimpanzees by immersing herself in their natural habitat. Instead of studying captive animals in zoos or conducting experiments in a lab, she spent years living among the chimpanzees in the forests of Gombe Stream National Park in Tanzania. This allowed her to observe their behavior, interactions, and lives up close, enabling her to understand them as both a species and individuals with emotions and bonds. The other options (A, B, and C) do not accurately describe Jane Goodall's approach to her research.

36. B. Body movements act as visual displays of emotion and intent.

Explanation: Jane Goodall observed that body movements of chimpanzees serve as visual displays of their emotions and intentions. She noted how gestures and body language were important means of communication among the chimpanzees. This observation highlighted the significance of non-verbal communication in their interactions. The other options (A, C, and D) do not accurately reflect Jane Goodall's observations about chimpanzee communication methods.

Grade 5 — Ans keys

37. A. They stripped twigs and made probes and chewed leaves to make sponges.

Explanation: According to Jane Goodall's observations, wild chimpanzees used tools by stripping twigs to make probes for fishing termites from their nests and chewing leaves to make sponges for getting water from shallow pools. This behavior demonstrated their ability to modify objects for specific purposes. The other options (B, C, and D) are not consistent with Jane Goodall's documented observations of chimpanzee tool use.

38. B. Conservationist

Explanation: Jane Goodall's current role is primarily that of a conservationist. While she is known for her pioneering work as a primatologist and her groundbreaking observations of chimpanzees in their natural habitat, she has also become a prominent advocate for wildlife conservation and habitat protection. Through her non-profit organization, the Jane Goodall Institute, she works to raise awareness and funds for the conservation of chimpanzees and their habitats, as well as other wildlife and environmental causes. While she has a background in anthropology, zoology, and primatology, her current focus and impact are most closely associated with her role as a conservationist.

39. C. She came to understand them as individuals with emotions and long-term bonds

Explanation: Jane Goodall's approach to studying chimpanzees was characterized by her deep immersion in their habitat and lives. Unlike traditional primatologists who studied captive animals in zoos, Goodall chose to observe chimpanzees in the wild, allowing her to experience their behavior and interactions up close. This approach enabled her to recognize them not just as a species, but as individual creatures with their own distinct personalities, emotions, and social relationships. This emphasis on understanding chimpanzees as unique individuals with emotions and long-term bonds was a significant departure from conventional scientific methods and contributed to her groundbreaking insights into their behavior and social dynamics.

40. A. Spent days observing and interacting with them

Explanation: Jane Goodall spent days alone in the forest observing and interacting with the chimpanzees. She immersed herself in their habitat, gradually gaining their trust and acceptance. Through her patient and dedicated presence, she was able to closely observe their behavior, interactions, and social dynamics, which formed the foundation of her groundbreaking research on chimpanzees. This hands-on approach allowed her to gather detailed insights into their lives and contributed to her profound understanding of their behavior as well as their individual personalities and emotions.

41. D. They were good toolmakers

Explanation: One of Jane Goodall's most surprising discoveries about wild chimpanzees was that they were good toolmakers. She observed that chimpanzees used objects as tools and often modified them to suit their purposes. For example, they stripped twigs to make probes for fishing termites from their nests and chewed leaves to make sponges for getting water from shallow pools. This discovery challenged the prevailing belief at the time that tool use was unique to humans and highlighted the complexity of chimpanzees' cognitive abilities and problem-solving skills. The other options (A, B, and C) are not mentioned in the passage and do not align with Goodall's observations and findings.

42. **D. Her present contributions**

Explanation: In this paragraph, the text discusses Jane Goodall's current role and contributions. It mentions how she championed the cause of chimpanzee conservation, launched an institution for wildlife research and conservation, and continues to work as a conservationist to raise awareness and funds for protecting chimpanzees and their habitats. This subheading accurately captures the focus of the paragraph, which is on Jane Goodall's ongoing efforts and contributions to the field of conservation. The other choices are incorrect because they do not accurately reflect the content of the paragraph: option A ("Jane's notebook") is not mentioned in the paragraph, option B ("Who is Jane Goodall?") is more general and not specific to the content, and option C ("Observations that Jane made about chimps") does not encompass the broader scope of Jane Goodall's current contributions beyond her observations.

THE WHITE TIGER

43. **C. Absence of the pigment pheomelanin**

Explanation: The cause of white fur in white Bengal tigers is the absence of the pigment pheomelanin. The passage explains that white Bengal tigers lack the pigment pheomelanin, which is present in Bengal tigers with orange-colored fur. This absence of pheomelanin results in the white fur of white Bengal tigers. The other choices are incorrect because they do not accurately describe the cause of the white fur in these tigers: option A ("Genetic mutation in other pigmentation genes") does not align with the information provided, and options B ("Exposure to sunlight for long durations") and D ("Excessive presence of pheomelanin") are not mentioned as causes in the passage.

44. **A. White Bengal tigers grow more quickly and heavily**

Explanation: According to the passage, white Bengal tigers have a propensity to grow more quickly and heavily than orange Bengal tigers. This information aligns with option a. The other choices are incorrect because they either present inaccurate information (options B and D) or do not reflect the comparison stated in the passage (option C).

45. **D. Inadequate camouflage due to their white colour fur**

Explanation: The passage mentions that white Bengal tigers are less able to follow prey or evade other predators because they lack adequate camouflage. This is due to their distinctive white fur, which makes them stand out in their environment. The other choices do not accurately explain the reason mentioned in the passage.

46. **D. Approximately once per 10,000 births**

Explanation: The passage states that the occurrence of white Bengal tigers in the wild is approximately once per 10,000 births. This makes them quite rare compared to other tigers with different fur coloring. The other choices provide incorrect frequency estimates.

47. **D. Increased probability of offspring with stripe-less phenotype**

Explanation: Prolonged inbreeding among white tigers can increase the probability of offspring with the stripe-less phenotype, as mentioned in the passage. The recessive gene responsible for this phenotype becomes homozygous due to continued inbreeding, leading to a higher likelihood of producing white tiger cubs without prominent stripes. Other choices do not accurately reflect the consequences of inbreeding discussed in the passage.

48. **a. Proneness**

Explanation: A synonym of 'propensity' is 'proneness.' Both words convey the idea of a natural inclination or tendency towards something. The other options do not have the same meaning as 'propensity.'

49. **A. Opaque and visible only in certain angles of light**

Explanation: Georges Cuvier described the stripes of the white tiger he observed as "opaque" and mentioned that they were only visible in certain angles of light. This suggests that the stripes were not easily distinguishable and required specific lighting conditions to become visible. The other options do not accurately capture Cuvier's description of the stripes.

50. **D. Para 4 & 5**

Explanation: Paragraph 4 talks about a second genetic disorder that can cause a tiger to have nearly no stripes at all, turning it almost completely white. It describes historical observations of a white variety of tiger with opaque stripes and no visible stripes except in certain angles of light. Paragraph 5 further discusses the breeding of contemporary white tigers with almost no stripes, explaining how the inbreeding of specific tigers led to the appearance of stripe-less individuals. Therefore, both paragraphs 4 and 5 address the anomaly of stripe less white tigers.

A Morning Adventure

1. B) The windows were encrusted with dirt

Explanation: In the story, the windows appeared dim despite the sunshine outside because they were covered with dirt. The passage mentions that the windows were so dirty that they would have made even bright sunlight seem faint. This is why the correct answer is B) The windows were encrusted with dirt. The other choices are incorrect because there is no mention of extreme cold (A), heavy fog outside (C), or tinted windows (D) as reasons for the dim appearance of the windows in the passage.

2. A) Go out for a walk

Explanation: Miss Jellyby suggests that they go out for a walk at that early hour in the morning. The passage states that although the morning was raw and the fog seemed heavy, Miss Jellyby proposed going out for a walk as a good idea. The other choices are incorrect because there is no mention of having breakfast (B), cleaning the windows (C), or taking a nap (D) as suggestions in the passage.

3. C) He skips breakfast and goes straight to the office

Explanation: Miss Jellyby describes her father's breakfast routine as him getting what he can and going to the office. The passage mentions that her father never has what you would call a regular breakfast, and sometimes there isn't even any milk for breakfast. This suggests that he skips breakfast and goes straight to the office. The other choices are incorrect because there is no mention of him having a regular breakfast (A), eating whatever is available (B), or having a preference for milk and bread (D) in the passage.

4. C) Dusty and messy

Explanation: When they came downstairs, the house was described as being in a dusty and messy condition. The passage mentions that the dinner-cloth had not been taken away and was left ready for breakfast. Crumbs, dust, and waste-paper were all over the house, indicating that the house was not clean and tidy. The other choices are incorrect because there is no mention of the house being cluttered with toys (B) or freshly painted (D) in the passage.

5. A) The public-house

Explanation: Before meeting the others, the cook went to the public-house. The passage mentions that the cook came out of a public-house, wiping her mouth as she passed by. This indicates that she had visited the public-house before encountering the others. The other choices are incorrect because there is no mention of the cook going to the grocery store (A), the bakery (C), or the park (D) in the passage.

6. B) Dawdle

Explanation: The word "dawdle" from paragraph 2 means 'to waste time.' In the passage, it is mentioned that breakfast is not ready for an hour afterwards because people dawdle, indicating that they waste time and delay. The other choices (A, C, D) do not mean 'to waste time' and are therefore incorrect.

7. C) The uncomfortable conditions indoors

Explanation: Miss Jellyby and the narrator decide to go for a walk in the morning because of the uncomfortable conditions indoors. The passage mentions that the morning was raw, the fog seemed heavy, and the windows were encrusted with dirt, making the indoor environment uncomfortable. This discomfort prompts them to go out for a walk. The other choices (A, B, D) are not mentioned as reasons for their decision to go for a walk in the passage and are therefore incorrect.

8. A) Because Peepy was covered in dirt and needed cleaning

Explanation: The narrator decides to wash Peepy because he was covered in dirt and needed cleaning. The passage mentions that the narrator made a proposal to Peepy to wash him, and Peepy submitted to the washing. There is no mention of Peepy requesting to be washed (B), a customary morning routine (C), or the house being too dirty (D) as reasons for the narrator's decision to wash Peepy.

A Useful Minister

9. D) He wanted to be far away from the outside scenes

Explanation: Tom was placed next to the aisle during the sermon because he wanted to be as far away as possible from the open window and the seductive outside summer scenes. The passage mentions that Tom was seated in a way that would prevent him from being easily distracted by the enticing scenes outside the window. The other choices (A, B, C) do not accurately capture the reason for Tom's placement next to the aisle in the passage.

10. B) The widow Douglas

Explanation: The "belle of the village" in the passage is described as the widow Douglas. The passage mentions her as fair, smart, and forty, with a generous and good-hearted nature, as well as being well-to-do. The other choices (A, C, D) do not fit the description of the "belle of the village" as provided in the passage.

11. C) He was good and was praised by everyone

Explanation: The boys in town hated Willie Mufferson because he was good and was praised by everyone. The passage mentions that he was the Model Boy, always taking careful care of his mother and being well-behaved, which made him the pride of all the matrons. This admiration and praise from adults likely led to jealousy and resentment from other boys. The other choices (A, B, D) do not accurately capture the reason for the boys' dislike of Willie Mufferson as mentioned in the passage.

12. B) He read it with strong emphasis on certain words

Explanation: The minister read the hymn in a peculiar style by beginning on a medium key and climbing steadily up until reaching a certain point, where he bore strong emphasis upon the topmost word, and then he plunged down as if from a spring-board. This unique and distinctive reading style is described in the passage. The other choices (A, C, D) do not accurately describe the peculiar style of reading the hymn as outlined in the passage.

13. C) The widow Douglas

Explanation: Among the congregation, the widow Douglas is described as generous, good-hearted, and well-to-do. The passage mentions her as fair, smart, and forty, with a generous, good-hearted soul, and being well-to-do. The other choices (A, B, D) do not fit the description of being generous, good-hearted, and well-to-do as provided in the passage.

14. D) They thought it was unnecessary and pretentious

Explanation: The boys thought having a handkerchief on Sundays made one a snob because they considered it unnecessary and pretentious. The passage mentions that Tom looked upon boys who had handkerchiefs as snobs, implying that he believed such an accessory was showy or affected. The other choices (A, B, C) do not accurately reflect the reason the boys thought having a handkerchief on Sundays made one a snob, as described in the passage.

15. A) 1

Explanation: In the context of the passage, the word "hospitable" is used to describe a person who is friendly and welcoming. It refers to the generous and warm nature of the widow Douglas. The second dictionary meaning "a suitable place" is not applicable to the way "hospitable" is used in this passage.

16. c) A suppressed laugh

Explanation: In paragraph 3, the word "tittering" refers to a suppressed or giggling kind of laugh. The passage mentions that the choir in the gallery was tittering and whispering, indicating that they were quietly laughing and exchanging comments. The other choices (A, B, D) do not accurately capture the meaning of "tittering" as used in the passage.

NORTHAMPTON

17. B) Proud and important

Explanation: Mrs. Norris felt proud and important about being the first to welcome the little girl. The passage mentions that she "regaled in the credit of being foremost to welcome her" and took pleasure in leading her into the others and recommending her to their kindness. This indicates that she took pride in her role and saw it as an opportunity to showcase her involvement and importance. The other choices (A, C, D) do not accurately capture Mrs. Norris's feelings as described in the passage.

18. C) He tried to be kind and conciliating.

Explanation: In the passage, it is mentioned that Sir Thomas tried to be all that was conciliating towards Fanny Price. He saw that she needed encouragement and made an effort to interact with her in a kind and friendly manner. The other choices (A, B, D) do not accurately describe how Sir Thomas interacted with Fanny Price as depicted in the passage.

19. B) With good humor and no embarrassment

Explanation: The passage mentions that the young people, specifically the sons who were seventeen and sixteen years old, sustained their share in the introduction very well. They treated their little cousin, Fanny Price, with good humor and no embarrassment. This indicates that they interacted with her in a friendly and comfortable manner. The other choices (A, C, D) do not accurately describe how the sons treated their little cousin as depicted in the passage.

20. A) They were younger and more fearful of their father.

Explanation: The passage mentions that the two girls were more at a loss during the introduction because they were younger and in greater awe of their father. Their father addressed them with particularity, which made them feel more uncomfortable and self-conscious. The other choices (B, C, D) do not accurately capture the reason for the girls being more at a loss compared to the boys, as described in the passage.

21. B) 2 years.

Explanation: There were two years between Fanny and the youngest cousin. This means they were not very far apart in age. The other choices (A, C, D) do not correctly state the age gap between Fanny and the youngest cousin.

22. A) She missed her home and felt ashamed of herself.

Explanation: The little girl was unhappy despite being told of her "wonderful good fortune" and the need to be happy because she missed her home and felt ashamed of herself. The passage mentions that Mrs. Norris had been talking to her about her good fortune and the expectation of gratitude and good behavior, which made her even more conscious of her misery. Additionally, the passage states that she longed for the home she had left. This indicates that her homesickness and sense of shame contributed to her unhappiness. The other choices (B, C, D) do not accurately capture the reasons for the little girl's unhappiness as described in the passage.

23. B) The daughters are younger and more attractive than Fanny.

Explanation: The passage describes the daughters as being decidedly handsome and well-grown, which implies that they are younger and more attractive than their cousin Fanny. This comparison is highlighted by the statement that education had given the daughters more confidence and address. The other choices (A, C D) do not accurately describe the comparison between the daughters' ages and appearances and Fanny's as presented in the passage.

24. B) Paragraph 2

Explanation: Paragraph 2 describes Fanny Price's physical appearance and demeanor when she first arrived at Northampton. It mentions her age, her small size, lack of striking beauty, timidity, shyness, and her shrinking from notice. It also mentions that her air, though awkward, was not vulgar, her voice was sweet, and her countenance was pretty when she spoke. The other choices (A, C, D) do not focus on describing Fanny Price's physical appearance and demeanor as depicted in paragraph 2.

25. C) prefix: en, suffix: ment

Explanation: The word "encouragement" is formed from a prefix "en-" (meaning "to cause to") and a suffix "-ment" (used to form nouns denoting an action or process). Therefore, the correct answer is option c) "prefix: en, suffix: ment." The other choices do not accurately represent the affixes in the word "encouragement."

The Coral Reef Ecosystem

26. B) Forming the hard coral skeleton.

Explanation: Coral polyps are primarily responsible for forming the hard coral skeleton in the coral reef ecosystem. The passage mentions that coral polyps secrete calcium carbonate, a process that results in the formation of the coral's robust skeleton. This skeleton serves as the structural framework of the entire reef. The other choices (A, C, D) do not accurately describe the primary role of coral polyps as depicted in the passage.

27. C) Because they exhibit similar levels of biodiversity as rainforests.

Explanation: Coral reefs are often referred to as "rainforests of the sea" because they exhibit similar levels of biodiversity as rainforests found on land. Just as rainforests on land are known for their incredible diversity of plant and animal species, coral reefs host a vast array of marine life, making them biodiversity hotspots in the ocean. The other choices (A, B, D) do not accurately capture the reason why coral reefs are called "rainforests of the sea" as depicted in the passage.

28. b) Algae provide corals with shelter and nutrients.

Explanation: The passage describes a mutualistic relationship between corals and algae (zooxanthellae), where the algae take residence within the coral tissues and perform photosynthesis, harnessing sunlight to produce energy and nutrients. In return, the corals provide the algae with a secure home and necessary substances. The other choices (A, C, D) do not accurately describe the mutualistic relationship between corals and algae as depicted in the passage.

29. Answer: C) It contributes to the structure and framework of the reef.

Explanation: The coral skeleton plays a role in the formation of a coral reef by contributing to the structure and framework of the reef. The passage mentions that coral polyps secrete calcium carbonate, which results in the formation of the coral's robust skeleton. Over time, these skeletons accumulate and collectively craft the structural framework of the entire reef. This skeletal framework provides the foundation upon which the diverse marine life and intricate architecture of the reef thrive. The other choices (A, B, D) do not accurately describe the role of the coral skeleton in the formation of a coral reef as depicted in the passage.

30. A) Coral reefs harbor the majority of marine species.

Explanation: Coral reefs are considered biodiversity hotspots because they host about a quarter of all marine species on the planet, despite covering only a fraction of the ocean floor. The incredible diversity of life found in coral reefs spans from the tiniest invertebrates to majestic marine mammals. This high concentration of diverse species in a relatively small area contributes to their status as biodiversity hotspots. The other choices (B, C, D) do not accurately describe the main reason why coral reefs are considered biodiversity hotspots as depicted in the passage.

31. D) Pollution resulting from coastal development and tourism.

Explanation: The passage identifies pollution resulting from coastal development and tourism as a significant threat to coral reefs. It mentions that tourist activities and coastal developments inflict physical damage, exacerbating the perilous situation of coral reefs. This pollution, originating both from land and sea, further deteriorates the health of the reefs. The other choices (A, B, C) are not specifically mentioned as significant threats to coral reefs in the passage.

32. D) By establishing marine protected areas and regulating human activities.

Explanation: Conservation efforts aim to protect and preserve coral reefs by establishing marine protected areas and regulating human activities. The passage mentions that organizations and governments collaborate to establish marine protected areas where stringent regulations limit human impact. Additionally, strategies to regulate fishing practices and reduce pollution are implemented to restore and sustain the delicate equilibrium of the reef ecosystem. While promoting awareness (C) is important, the primary focus of conservation efforts, as described in the passage, is on establishing protected areas and regulating human activities (D). The other choices (A, B) are not mentioned as methods of conservation efforts in the passage.

33. C) Climate change and human activities

Explanation: The primary cause of coral bleaching and decline in reef health, as mentioned in the passage, is climate change and human activities. Climate change, driven by rising temperatures and ocean acidification, poses a significant threat to coral reefs. Additionally, human activities such as overfishing, pollution, tourist activities, and coastal development contribute to the deterioration of reef health. The other choices (A, B, D) do not accurately describe the primary cause of coral bleaching and decline in reef health as depicted in the passage.

The Inspiring Journey of Mahatma Gandhi

34. D) To challenge the salt tax imposed by the British

Explanation: The main purpose of the Salt March led by Mahatma Gandhi in 1930 was to challenge the salt tax imposed by the British. The passage mentions that Gandhi led a 240-mile-long march to the Arabian Sea, symbolically making salt from seawater as an act of civil disobedience. This protest aimed to challenge the oppressive British salt tax and inspired millions of Indians to join the freedom movement. The other choices (A, B, C) do not accurately describe the main purpose of the Salt March as depicted in the passage.

35. B) A movement to boycott British goods and promote Indian products

Explanation: The "Swadeshi Movement" promoted by Gandhi during India's struggle for independence was a movement to boycott British goods and promote Indian products. The passage mentions that Gandhi promoted the use of traditional Indian spinning wheels, or "charkhas," to produce handmade cloth, urging people to boycott British textiles. This movement aimed to strengthen India's economy and foster a sense of national pride by encouraging the use of locally made products and reducing dependence on British goods. The other choices (A, C, D) do not accurately describe the "Swadeshi Movement" as depicted in the passage.

36. C) Persistent

Explanation: The word "relentless" means showing no pity or mercy, and in this context, it refers to Gandhi's unwavering determination and persistence in his pursuit of truth and India's independence. Among the given options, "persistent" is a synonym for "relentless," as it also implies a continuous and determined effort. The other choices (A, B, D) do not accurately capture the meaning of "relentless."

37. C) Aggression

Explanation: The philosophy of "ahimsa" or non-violence, as advocated by Gandhi, is about refraining from causing harm or violence to others. The opposite of this philosophy would be "aggression," which refers to hostile or violent behavior. The other choices (A, B, D) are positive qualities that may align with Gandhi's philosophy of non-violence, rather than being its opposite.

38. A) To promote the use of traditional Indian textiles.

Explanation: Gandhi encouraged Indians to boycott British goods and institutions as part of the "Swadeshi Movement." The passage mentions that he promoted the use of traditional Indian spinning wheels, or "charkhas," to produce handmade cloth, urging people to boycott British textiles. The aim was to promote the use of locally made Indian products, such as textiles, and reduce dependence on British goods. This choice aligns with Gandhi's emphasis on self-reliance and promoting traditional Indian practices. The other choices (B, C, D) do not accurately reflect the reason for Gandhi's encouragement to boycott British goods and institutions as described in the passage.

39. C) Disobedience

Explanation: "Satyagraha" is Gandhi's philosophy of non-violent resistance, which involves passive resistance to unjust laws and practices. The term "disobedience" is often used interchangeably with "Satyagraha" because both concepts involve defying authority or laws through non-violent means. The other choices (A, B, D) do not accurately capture the essence of "Satyagraha" as described in the passage.

40. D) His decision to fast in response to India's partition.

Explanation: Gandhi's decision to fast in response to India's partition demonstrates his commitment to stopping violence and promoting communal harmony. The passage mentions that Gandhi undertook a fast until all parties agreed to peace and communal harmony to prevent the communal violence that resulted from the partition of India. This choice aligns with Gandhi's principles of non-violence and his efforts to bring about unity and harmony even in the face of challenging circumstances. The other choices (A, B, C) are significant events in Gandhi's life and work, but they do not specifically highlight his commitment to stopping violence and promoting communal harmony as the fasting incident does.

41. C) Gandhi's experiences with racial discrimination.

Explanation: The title "Gandhi's Early Life and Education" suggests that the main focus of the 2nd paragraph is on Gandhi's early life and educational experiences. The paragraph specifically mentions his time in South Africa, where he witnessed racial discrimination against Indians and became interested in fighting for civil rights and social justice. This choice accurately reflects the content of the paragraph and the emphasis on Gandhi's experiences with racial discrimination during his early years. The other choices (A, B, D) do not fully capture the main focus of the paragraph as suggested by the title.

"Wake, Little Brother; I bring news."

42. A) He is badly injured in a fight

Explanation: In the passage, it is mentioned that Shere Khan has gone away to hunt far off till his coat grows again because he is badly singed. This indicates that Shere Khan has been injured in a fight or encounter, which has resulted in him being badly singed and needing time to recover. Therefore, option a) "He is badly injured in a fight" accurately describes the reason for Shere Khan's departure. The other options (B, C, D) do not accurately reflect the information provided in the passage regarding Shere Khan's condition.

43. D) To always remember his wolf family

Explanation: In the passage, when Gray Brother brings news to Mowgli, he reminds Mowgli about the threat from Shere Khan and asks if Mowgli will forget his wolf family because of the influence of men. Mowgli replies, "Never. I will always remember that I love thee and all in our cave." This indicates that Mowgli has made a promise to always remember and cherish his wolf family. The other options (A, B, C) do not accurately reflect the promise that Mowgli has made in this context.

44. C) He knows it's wrong to harm others

Explanation: In the passage, it is mentioned that Mowgli is angered by the village children making fun of him and teasing him. However, despite his anger, Mowgli refrains from picking them up and breaking them in two. This restraint is attributed to his knowledge of the Law of the Jungle, which emphasizes the importance of keeping one's temper and not harming others. Therefore, Mowgli's resistance to harming the village children stems from his understanding that it is morally wrong to cause harm to others. The other options (A, B, D) do not capture the primary reason for Mowgli's restraint in this context.

45. C) Herd the buffaloes while they graze

Explanation: In the passage, it is mentioned that the village head-man tells Mowgli that he will have to go out with the buffaloes the next day and herd them while they graze. This indicates that Mowgli's task is to take care of the buffaloes and ensure that they graze safely. The other options (A, B, D) are not specifically mentioned in relation to the village head-man's request to Mowgli.

46. A) Wild animals stealing crops

Explanation: In the passage, it is mentioned that the deer and the wild pig grubbed up the villagers' crops, and occasionally, the tiger carried off a man at twilight within sight of the village gates. This indicates that wild animals stealing crops and posing a threat to the village is a common occurrence. The other options (B, C, D) are not specifically mentioned as common threats to the village in the context of the passage.

47. C) Faintest

Explanation: In paragraph 9, the word "faintest" is used to indicate something that is very slight or barely perceptible. In the given context, it refers to Mowgli having no idea about the difference or distinction between castes and how it affects people's social status. The word "faintest" suggests a lack of clarity or understanding. The other options (A, B, D) do not convey the meaning of "indefinite" or "unclear" in this context.

48. B) Paragraph 4

Explanation: Paragraph 4 describes Mowgli's return to India and his willingness to learn about human ways. It mentions how he became a prominent leader in the Indian National Congress and advocated for various rights. This paragraph also mentions his encouragement for Indians to boycott British goods and institutions. It focuses on Mowgli's interaction with the villagers and his efforts to challenge British colonial rule using non-violent methods. The other options (A, C, D) do not primarily focus on Mowgli's willingness to learn about human ways and his interaction with the villagers.

49. C) He liked being part of village discussions.

Explanation: In paragraph 9, it is mentioned that Mowgli was pleased after being appointed a servant of the village because he could join the village club under the fig-tree. This club was where the old men of the village gathered to talk, share tales, and discuss various matters. Mowgli's eagerness to be a part of this club and participate in the discussions suggests that he felt pleased about this aspect of his role in the village. The other options (A, B, D) are not explicitly mentioned as reasons for his pleasure in the passage.

50. D) "Nighttime Conversations"

Explanation: The last paragraph of the passage describes the activities of the village club, where the old men of the village gather under a fig-tree to smoke, talk, and share tales. The paragraph emphasizes the storytelling and discussions that take place in this nighttime gathering. The title "Nighttime Conversations" captures the essence of this paragraph and the atmosphere of the village club. The other options (A, B, C) do not fully encapsulate the focus of the paragraph on the conversations and stories shared during these gatherings.

Made in the USA
Columbia, SC
04 March 2025